CYCLING CLIMBS OF SCOTLAND

A ROAD CYCLIST'S GUIDE

SIMON WARREN

F

FRANCES
LINCOLN

Frances Lincoln Limited
A subsidiary of Quarto Publishing Group UK
74–77 White Lion Street
London N1 9PF

Cycling Climbs of Scotland: A Road Cyclist's Guide

First Frances Lincoln edition 2017

A catalogue record for this book is available from the British Library.

978-0-7112-3709-4

Printed and bound in China

1 2 3 4 5 6 7 8 9

Quarto is the authority on a wide range of topics.

Quarto educates, entertains and enriches the lives of
our readers – enthusiasts and lovers of hands-on living.

www.QuartoKnows.com

MIX
Paper from
responsible sources
FSC® C016973

Thanks to my family and friends for their continued support
and patience, and in particular to my Dad, who accompanied me on my
research trips – two weeks of wild weather, birdwatching, vicious hills,
and single malts. Thanks also to all the Strava users and Twitter
followers who have suggested climbs for me to seek out, especially
Duncan Firth for leading me to a couple of absolute belters.

CONTENTS

Northern Highlands

HIGHLANDS

Great Glen

Grampian Mountains

EAST SCOTLAND

WEST SCOTLAND

Central Lowlands

SOUTHERN SCOTLAND

Southern Uplands

P5
INTRODUCTION

P12
HIGHLANDS

P54
EAST SCOTLAND

P86
WEST SCOTLAND

P112
SOUTHERN SCOTLAND

P140
CHECKLIST

SCOTLAND

Back in 2013, my father accompanied me on an epic research trip for *100 Greatest Cycling Climbs of the Tour de France*. We crossed the Pyrenees from west to east and, as I bagged mountain climbs, he indulged his passion for bird watching; while I battled the Col du Tourmalet, he – aged 75 – went in search of the last of the season's Snow Buntings. On the journey from the gruelling slopes of the Port de Larrau and the vicious Col de Marie-Blanque

all the way to Andorra, accompanied by soaring Lammergeiers, we were both like pigs in mud.

It was the perfect trip, so when I was planning my research for this book, I knew he would want to join me. Together with mountains, Scotland is home to not just one, but two types of eagle. It wasn't just the prospect of spotting raptors that lured him in, though, he was also keen to revisit the many places he had ventured to in the area as a young man. There was not a

loch we passed or a glen we crossed that he didn't have a story about. Back in his youth, with just a few jumpers on their backs, he and his mates would take the train from the Black Country into the Highlands to camp in old canvas tents in the harsh wilderness. Equipped with little else but a thirst for adventure, they were a bunch of intrepid birdwatchers with a passion that few could stand in the way of. Today, Scotland still presents many of the same opportunities for exploration, and thankfully the clothing needed for it is much improved. On quiet roads and under giant skies, you can ride beneath towering peaks, surrounded by nature and blissfully removed from modernity.

Much like on our trip to the Pyrenees, each day I would ride mountains while Dad tramped off into the woods. However, in Scotland we would end the day by indulging in our shared love of whisky. Whisky comes alive in Scotland – when you have a glass of Talisker on the Isle of Skye, it is like drinking the blood of the island. We insisted on sampling the local tipple in every town we stopped in – in one sip, we were instantly connected to the land, the water, the peat, and the weather. Oh yes, the weather… I should probably mention the weather. Did we have any rain, you wonder? Just a bit! Researching *100 Greatest Cycling Climbs* and its sequel, I did not see clear sky once. And by day five of the first research trip for this book, it felt like I had been living under the sea. With one day left, I had zero kit remaining, and my best efforts to

turn the hotel room into a giant airing cupboard hadn't worked. The car stank, my shoes squelched, and the bike was hidden under a film of dirt – it almost broke me. But then came the second trip. Admittedly, we had a damp first day, but the forecast for the following few was very optimistic. The next morning, eyes closed, I tentatively drew back the curtains. I was almost too scared to look; I wanted an empty sky, I wanted dry feet, I wanted to be able to take a picture without having to shield the camera from a constant stream of drizzle. Slowly, I opened my eyes... A miracle! The curse had been broken. The sky was a deep blue and the morning was awash with sunlight. I immediately got my kit on, woke up Dad, and told him I would be back for breakfast. In the early

morning light I rode up Fairlie Moor (page 106), and the views out over the ocean were incredible. Scotland may be beautiful in the rain, but it is off-the-scale fantastic in the sun.

For the next three days I was able to wear the same pair of cycling shoes and I didn't have to wrap everything in endless plastic bags to keep the moisture out. Best of all, I could concentrate on putting some proper effort into the climbs.

And what climbs they are, running all the way from the windswept Western Isles, across the Highlands and into the agriculturally rich east Scotland. Do not be put off by the conditions, and do be excited by the open spaces and clean air. With this book as your guide, head north and keep heading north until the South is just a dot on the horizon.

PASSING
PLACE

THE
REMOTE
PART

In the early 1990s one of my favourite bands was the Scottish outfit Idlewild. Drawn to their unbridled energy and explosive live shows, my future wife and I managed to catch them seven times in one summer. Their first two albums were packed to the gills with short eruptions of violent yet melodic anthems, but such youthful bursts of energy, like the mayfly, rarely last long. Nevertheless, they did not fade away completely – they evolved and returned with their third album, *The Remote Part*, and a masterpiece of music in the track 'Scottish Fiction'. Starting gently and building up to a euphoric finale, it painted in sound an

of the modern world lift from your shoulders; the air becomes fresher, the pace of life is slower, the roads are clearer, and the weather is wilder. Yes, it can be hostile up there, especially on the west coast, but a wise man once said: 'There is no such thing as bad weather, only unsuitable clothing.' Or something like that. On the approach to the first climb in this book, over Quinag mountain, the purity of the landscape and its exquisite ruggedness are simply stunning. Every stubborn blade of grass that withstands the howling winds, every exposed rock that has been worn bare from years of exposure to the elements is a jewel. And the roads: the

'We stop in every passing place, to watch the world move faster than we do'

Idlewild, 2002

epic vision of the simplicity, the space, and, of course, the remoteness of the Highlands*. For many years, 'the remote part' for me was just a picture in my mind, the lyrics in a song. That was until I ventured north of Fort William and deep into Sutherland where I, at last, experienced it in the flesh.

I have travelled a fair bit in subsequent years and been to a few remote parts of the globe, but all of these have required a long haul flight to get to. But the Scottish Highlands, no matter where you are in the British Isles, are just a (sometimes very long) car drive away. And the further north you travel, the more you feel the weight

roads are amazing. They are empty and quiet, sweeping and flowing their way through hills and valleys, connecting far-flung villages and towns. They are freedom, and they are adventure.

After living in London for over 20 years, it is very easy to become London-centric. But up in Sutherland, London might as well be on a different planet. It is crazy to think that two such drastically different environments inhabit the same tiny island. So whether you are looking for hills, or just an escape, I urge you to leave your towns and cities, to pack your best waterproofs and warmest base layers, and head north, to The Remote Part.

*Of course, the song is actually about a girl.

REMEMBER to check your bike, check your body, wear a helmet, and, above all, have fun!

LEGEND

UNDERSTANDING THE FACTFILE AND RATINGS

LOCATIONS

You will be able to locate each hill from the small maps provided: simply, **S** marks the start and **F** marks the finish. I would suggest you invest in either Ordnance Survey maps or a GPS system to help plan your routes in more detail. The grid reference in the Factfile locates the summit of each climb, and in brackets is the relevant **OS Landranger** map. The graphic at the start of each chapter will show you where the hills lie in the context of each region.

TIMINGS

Each Factfile includes the approximate time needed to ride each hill. Timed over the distance marked, this is how long it took me to complete each climb at a reasonable but comfortable pace. Since I rode in all weathers, from blizzards to baking heat, I have adjusted the times slightly to accommodate for the adverse conditions I faced on the day. The times could be used as a target but are really just intended to help you plan your rides.

FACTFILE

WHERE Head south out of Aviemore on the B9152 then turn south-east on the B970. At Coylumbridge turn on to the road to the Glenmore Forest Park, pass the lodge, and then climb.

GRID REF NH 989 062 (**OS36**)

LENGTH 5400m

HEIGHT GAIN 300m

APPROX CLIMB TIME 22.5mins

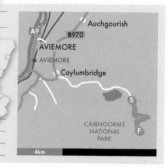

RATINGS

The climbs are rated from **1/10** to **10/10** within the context of the book. The rating is an amalgamation of gradient, length, the likely hostility of the riding conditions, and the condition of the surface. All the climbs are tough, therefore **1/10** equals 'hard', and **10/10** equals 'it's all you can do to keep your bike moving'. Some will suit you more than others; the saying 'horses for courses' applies, but all the **10/10** climbs will test any rider.

MAP KEY

Motorway	M1
A Road	A123
B Road	B1234
Minor Road	
Rail line	STATION
Hill route	S START / F FINISH
Town	TOWN
Scale	2km

HIGHLANDS

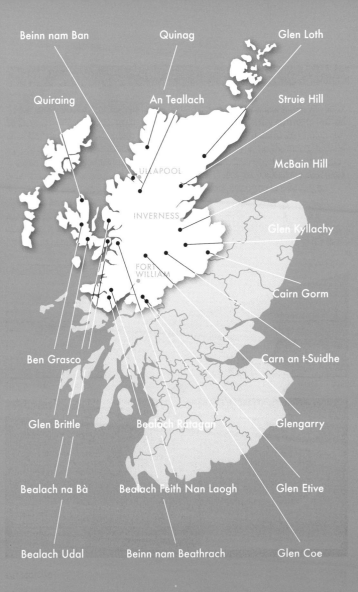

Beinn nam Ban

Quinag

Glen Loth

Quiraing

An Teallach

Struie Hill

ULLAPOOL

McBain Hill

INVERNESS

Glen Kyllachy

FORT
WILLIAM

Ben Grasco

Cairn Gorm

Carn an t-Suidhe

Glen Brittle

Glengarry

Bealach Ratagan

Bealach na Bà

Glen Etive

Bealach Udal

Bealach Feith Nan Laogh

Beinn nam Beathrach

Glen Coe

RATING
5/10

QUINAG

UNAPOOL, SUTHERLAND

Sutherland makes the most remote parts of England look like a well-tended garden. It is utterly rugged, totally wild, and deathly quiet. It also marks the northernmost point of my travels, and the journey was certainly worth it. Arriving at the base of Quinag I first tackled the southern side, before descending and tackling this ascent (which, in my opinion, is the better of the two). Rising from Unapool, the start of the climb is nasty up to an easing past the turning to the B869, then you hit some more sharp slopes. After meandering for a while you bend left, cross a small brow, and then ahead will see some switchbacks cut into the primitive vista. Steep enough to force you from the saddle, but not to grind you to a halt, they bend first right then harder left, cutting up through the rocks. Heading away from the bends you line up for the top and this is where the wind can hit you so, although the gradient fades, it can still be a real fight to the summit.

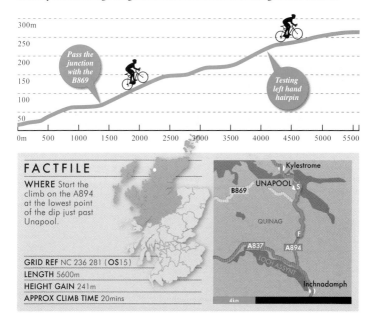

Pass the junction with the B869

Testing left hand hairpin

FACTFILE

WHERE Start the climb on the A894 at the lowest point of the dip just past Unapool.

GRID REF NC 236 281 (**OS**15)

LENGTH 5600m

HEIGHT GAIN 241m

APPROX CLIMB TIME 20mins

Kylestrome

UNAPOOL

B869

QUINAG

A837   A894

LOCH ASSYNT

Inchnadamph

4km

GLEN LOTH

LOTHMORE, SUTHERLAND

With a significant bit of downhill after two kilometres, I considered starting this climb further from the main road, but then the opening is such a shock to the system that it would be a shame not to include it. Ramping up directly from the A9, past various signs warning of snowdrifts and other likely perils, its killer beginning is soon behind you, then you drop down and cross a small stream. From here it is a rough old road – in fact, it probably has more turf along its central ridge than some lower league football pitches. Add this to the mounds of animal waste and abundance of potholes and I can safely say it is not one for your best tyres. Once past the summit the road also turns to gravel, so be warned. The pitch of the slope ebbs and flows in the shadow of the hills to your left, always a struggle but never a chore, all the way to the brow where you are treated to breathtaking views of the stunning Scottish landscape.

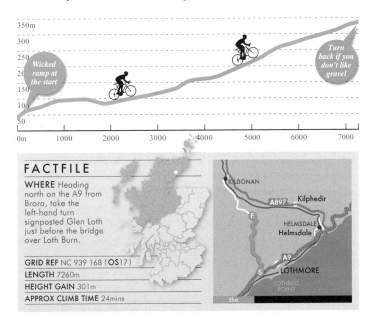

Wicked ramp at the start

Turn back if you don't like gravel

FACTFILE

WHERE Heading north on the A9 from Brora, take the left-hand turn signposted Glen Loth just before the bridge over Loth Burn.

GRID REF NC 939 168 (**OS**17)

LENGTH 7260m

HEIGHT GAIN 301m

APPROX CLIMB TIME 24mins

KILDONAN
A897 Kilphedir
HELMSDALE
Helmsdale
A9
LOTHMORE
LOTHBEG POINT

BEINN NAM BAN

BADRALLACH, ROSS AND CROMARTY

While scanning my map I spotted this road connecting the small village of Badrallach with the outside world – a quieter road I may never find. This dead end, tucked away on a tiny peninsula on Scotland's rugged west coast, is also home to two cracking little climbs. Unfortunately for your legs the better of the pair is the rise up from Badrallach, so you will have to ride all the way over from Dundonnell House first, then drop down and turn back around before you can attempt it. The early slopes are not too punishing and come in steps: tough for a bit, backing off, then hard again. As a few kinks appear in the climb's course the gradient begins to sting the legs, and the roughly-surfaced road, likely populated by sheep, starts to bend left. Past this subtle change in direction it is a real battle, with two severe ramps punctuated by a brief lull up to the hairpin, where you must continue round to reach the summit at the brow.

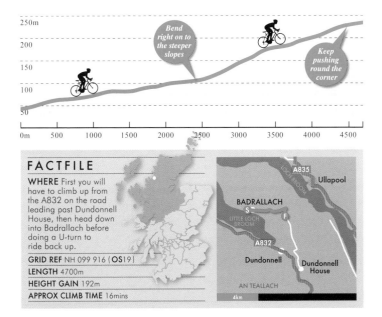

Bend right on to the steeper slopes

Keep pushing round the corner

FACTFILE

WHERE First you will have to climb up from the A832 on the road leading past Dundonnell House, then head down into Badrallach before doing a U-turn to ride back up.

GRID REF NH 099 916 (OS19)

LENGTH 4700m

HEIGHT GAIN 192m

APPROX CLIMB TIME 16mins

AN TEALLACH

DUNDONNELL, ROSS AND CROMARTY

Lengthwise, this climb is almost up there with some of the great Alpine passes but, whereas they tend to climb 1,000 metres over a similar distance, this one racks up a more modest 330 metres. Heading away from the shores of Little Loch Broom the first three kilometres are a breeze – you might even risk the big ring – but once you reach the large, orange snow gates it begins to ramp up, so change down. Stiff for just over a kilometre the climb then allows you a short rest before you hit the long middle section. Now in the wide, open valley you will see the road snake into the distance on a substantial 7% gradient. Arcing round to the left it is a formidable challenge up to a passing between huge rocks, where the steeper slopes end. On the whole the final four kilometres to the top are gentle, with a couple of nasty steep bits thrown in before the summit, which is not where you think it is, but in fact 1,500 metres further on.

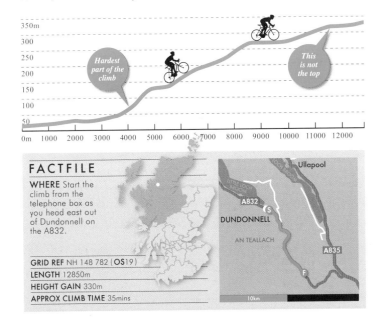

Hardest part of the climb

This is not the top

FACTFILE

WHERE Start the climb from the telephone box as you head east out of Dundonnell on the A832.

GRID REF	NH 148 782 (OS19)
LENGTH	12850m
HEIGHT GAIN	330m
APPROX CLIMB TIME	35mins

STRUIE HILL

It rained so hard when I rode this climb that all I wanted to do was get to the top and away from it, which is a shame as it is a cracking little road. Start where the B9176 forks gently away from the A836 and the upper shores of the Dornoch Firth, and head into the forest. The first kilometre will warm the legs up nicely, then there's a 90-degree right-hand bend followed by a slight dip, after which the gradient increases again. Winding through the trees you reach a sign advertising a viewpoint in one mile, but it is further than this to the top. Up next there is another slight drop and the road snakes across a high stone bridge before entering a sweeping left-hand curve and straightening up. From here the slope is a uniform 7% gradient across the heather-covered hillside overlooking the estuary. Head on, past the viewpoint, and continue climbing round to the right to find the summit where the road plateaus.

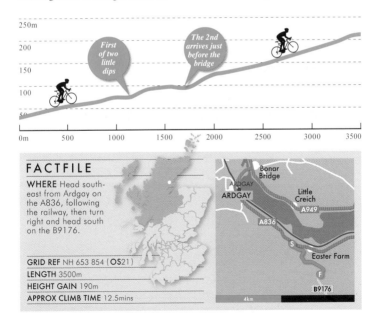

First of two little dips

The 2nd arrives just before the bridge

FACTFILE

WHERE Head south-east from Ardgay on the A836, following the railway, then turn right and head south on the B9176.

GRID REF NH 653 854 (OS21)

LENGTH 3500m

HEIGHT GAIN 190m

APPROX CLIMB TIME 12.5mins

Bonar Bridge

ARDGAY

ARDGAY

Little Creich

A949

A836

S

Easter Farm

F

B9176

4km

RATING

11/10

BEALACH NA BÀ

This is it: the Holy Grail. The toughest and wildest climb in Britain. Believe the hype – anything you have read or been told about this amazing road is true. Leave the head of Loch Kishorn, turn left, and you are on your way, rolling past the signs advertising the various dangers that lie ahead. It's not too steep to begin with but, as the road bends hard left at the base of an almighty tower of rock, the torment starts. Now climbing steeply the slither of rough road clinging precariously to the mountainside bends hard right to deliver you into true wilderness. Up ahead the final bends come into view, but there is an endless, soul-destroying 20% slope to tackle before you reach them. Once you arrive at the four hairpins they may seem too much, but fear not, between each one you are allowed a slight rest to recover for the next. Zig-zag past the cascading waterfalls to exit this infamous tangle of tarmac, rounding one final bend to finish.

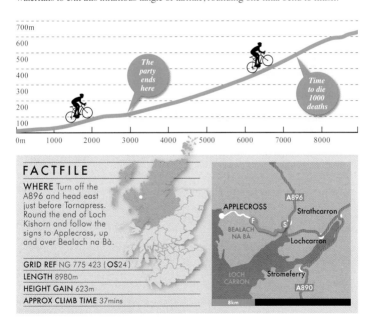

FACTFILE

WHERE Turn off the A896 and head east just before Tornapress. Round the end of Loch Kishorn and follow the signs to Applecross, up and over Bealach na Bà.

GRID REF NG 775 423 (**OS**24)

LENGTH 8980m

HEIGHT GAIN 623m

APPROX CLIMB TIME 37mins

RATING
6/10

QUIRAING

BROGAIG, ISLE OF SKYE

Atop the Isle of Skye lies a road so stunning you will never want it to end – the grandeur of its final bends have few peers in these isles. Starting at the junction with the A855 it is steep from the get-go, rising up and away from the scattered houses of Brogaig. Take care to stay right at a confusing junction and continue to climb up to a cattle grid. After this the road levels and you cross a plateau beneath the jagged peaks of Quiraing. Bumping up and down slightly, you pass a small cemetery before reaching a hard, straight 15% stretch to some fantastic corners at the top. First left, rocks jutting up either side of you, boulders strewn along the roadside, then right into the hardest stretch of climbing. Although not even this will spoil your enjoyment of these bends, set in their own natural amphitheatre. Finally, you turn sharp left and all too soon the gradient eases and you reach the summit where you are simply left wanting more.

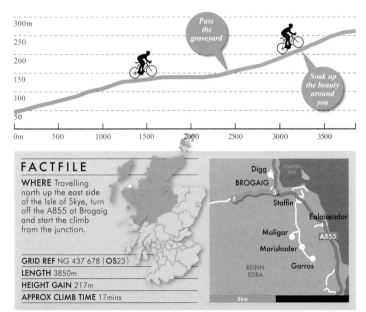

FACTFILE

WHERE Travelling north up the east side of the Isle of Skye, turn off the A855 at Brogaig and start the climb from the junction.

GRID REF NG 437 678 (**OS**23)

LENGTH 3850m

HEIGHT GAIN 217m

APPROX CLIMB TIME 17mins

RATING
5/10

BEN GRASCO

PORTREE, ISLE OF SKYE

Reaching deep into the interior of Skye, and well off the beaten track linking the small village of Glenmore with the road to Portree, this rugged, exposed, crumbling-at-the-edges climb is perfect Scotland. You are very unlikely to encounter much evidence of human life during your ascent, which for the first kilometre heads in pretty much a straight line. You will also be able to spot almost the whole road snaking across the hillside in front of you as the gradient picks up to and settles on a tough but not overwhelming 8%. Don't worry, it will get steeper soon. As you ride, wallowing in the wonder of the raw natural beauty around you, you hit the first of three distinct bends – arcing steep right, it is a shock to the legs. Vicious at the apex it delivers you to an equally tough left-hand bend followed by another right-hand hairpin from where it is just a few hundred metres to the passing place at the empty summit.

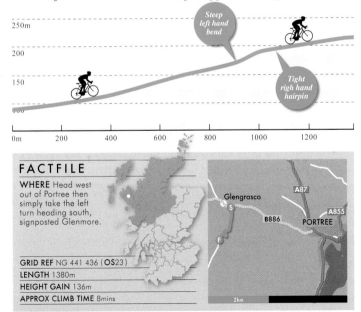

FACTFILE

WHERE Head west out of Portree then simply take the left turn heading south, signposted Glenmore.

GRID REF NG 441 436 (OS23)

LENGTH 1380m

HEIGHT GAIN 136m

APPROX CLIMB TIME 8mins

GLEN BRITTLE

BUALINTUR, ISLE OF SKYE

As you head down to the bottom of this road make sure you take the time to soak up the views. That way you can focus on the climb and nothing but the climb on the way back up. Linking the small village of Bualintur with the rest of the island, there is a long flat stretch from the coast through the wonderful Glenbrittle. Then, when you cross the River Brittle, you begin to gain altitude. Ahead of you the road rises, tracing the edge of the trees on the hillside as it bends slightly left. Passing a car park on the approach to a pair of bends the slope now starts to hurt. Climbing steeply the first corner swings left then the next turns hard right, where you hit the worst part of the climb on the exit through rough grassland. Once you have tackled the second corner the slope eases dramatically, so stick it in the big ring to really wind it up all the way to the brow.

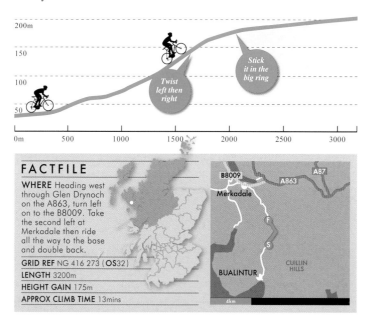

Twist left then right

Stick it in the big ring

FACTFILE

WHERE Heading west through Glen Drynoch on the A863, turn left on to the B8009. Take the second left at Merkadale then ride all the way to the base and double back.

GRID REF NG 416 273 (**OS**32)

LENGTH 3200m

HEIGHT GAIN 175m

APPROX CLIMB TIME 13mins

BEALACH UDAL

KYLERHEA, ISLE OF SKYE

Some of the climbs in this book are a little out of the way, and some like this one lie at the end of a long, convoluted dead end. But trust me, you want to make the effort to find this one. In fact, it is so good I would have cut through a forest of thorns and carried my bike over hot coals to reach it. Unless you take the ferry from the mainland to the base you will have the pleasure of descending it first, all the way down to the jetty, before turning around to climb back up. The start is pretty hard, then it gets easier through the scattered houses of Kylerhea. For a couple of kilometres it rises steadily, never really testing you, but the real fun awaits… The last kilometre is an utter brute – hugging the hillside, a rusting barrier the only thing shielding you from the sheer drop on your left, it hits 20% and sticks to it. You will see a brow but it is not the top – it backs off a touch and then ramps up again. If it wasn't so utterly awesome, it might just hurt.

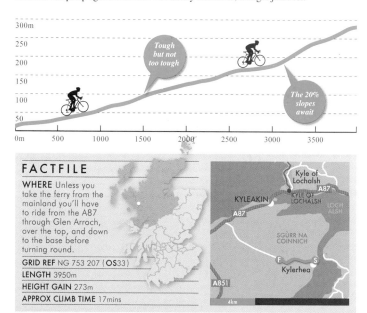

Tough but not too tough

The 20% slopes await

FACTFILE

WHERE Unless you take the ferry from the mainland you'll have to ride from the A87 through Glen Arroch, over the top, and down to the base before turning round.

GRID REF NG 753 207 (**OS**33)

LENGTH 3950m

HEIGHT GAIN 273m

APPROX CLIMB TIME 17mins

RATING 8/10

BEALACH RATAGAN

RATAGAN, LOCHALSH

This magnificent road is the spitting image of many a mountain pass – the Col du Télégraphe in France springs to mind. Begin from the cattle grid on the flat plain on the southern edge of Loch Duich and head up the rugged surface past the turning to Ratagan. After the turn, the surface worsens, but it clears up as the narrow road heads inland and away from the shores of the loch. The climb sweeps its way between tall dark conifers and you will soon have to start clicking down the gears as the slope approaches 15%. After a sharp hairpin right, things ease back for a while, before you are forced into a huge, steep, left-hand bend. After this there's another right-hand turn and then it is hard going, out of the saddle all the way up to the point where the road turns left to a viewpoint. Pause for a moment to take in the majestic views of the mountains reflected in the loch, and then head right to roll to the finish at a passing place.

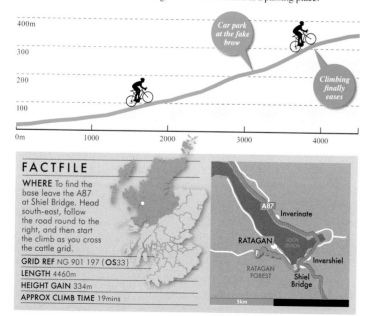

Car park at the fake brow

Climbing finally eases

400m
300
200
100
0m   1000   2000   3000   4000

FACTFILE

WHERE To find the base leave the A87 at Shiel Bridge. Head south-east, follow the road round to the right, and then start the climb as you cross the cattle grid.

GRID REF NG 901 197 (**OS**33)

LENGTH 4460m

HEIGHT GAIN 334m

APPROX CLIMB TIME 19mins

A87
Inverinate
RATAGAN
LOCH DUICH
F
RATAGAN
FOREST
Invershiel
S
Shiel Bridge
5km

GLENGARRY

INVERGARRY, LOCHABER

Set on the A87, the main road linking Invergarry with Kyle of Lochalsh, this is one of the busier roads in the book, but this being the Scottish Highlands, you will never face too much traffic. Start the climb as the smooth wide road leaves the shores of Loch Garry, twisting right and then left. This is a very gentle climb, almost a big ring climb, as the gradient stays in single figures the whole way up. Weaving ever upwards through the forested lower slopes you reach the Glengarry viewpoint at about halfway. From here the tree cover is sparser, revealing stunning views out over the loch but also leaving you a little more exposed to the wind as the long trail of tarmac snakes its way across the hillside. Heading ever so slightly right through a multitude of sweeping bends you eventually bend sharp right to arrive, without fanfare, at the car park on the cairn-littered summit.

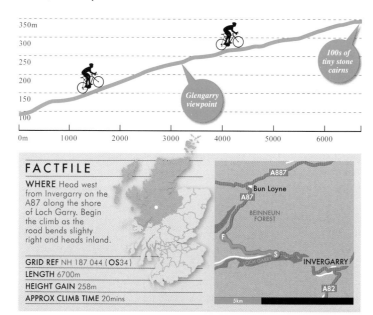

Glengarry viewpoint

100s of tiny stone cairns

FACTFILE

WHERE Head west from Invergarry on the A87 along the shore of Loch Garry. Begin the climb as the road slighty right and heads inland.

GRID REF NH 187 044 (**OS**34)

LENGTH 6700m

HEIGHT GAIN 258m

APPROX CLIMB TIME 20mins

BEALACH FEITH NAN LAOGH

STRONTIAN, LOCHABER

This climb takes a while to get going, but stick with it because at the end of the rainbow lies pure climbing gold. Starting as the road bends left at the left turn to Ariundle, it is tough for a while, but then it eases as you pass by the houses dotted on the hillside. After every stretch of climbing there is somewhere to recover – up a bit, levelling, then up a bit more. Across a cattle grid the road takes you past the final buildings and into what you came to find: a myriad of steep bends cutting their way through the harsh rocky landscape. After the first batch you come to the base of a leg-breaking straight that gets steeper and steeper. There is a brief easing round the corner at the top and then it gets steeper still, up to 1-in-4, before turning left. Here you have a chance to survey what you have conquered. Switching back, right then left, the last stretch is uphill all the way to the peak, next to an antenna on the brow.

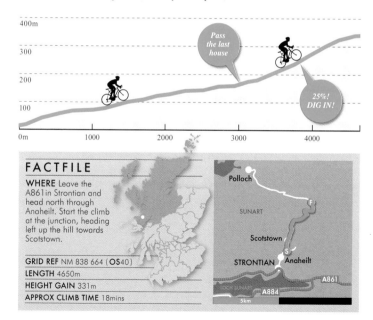

Pass the last house

25%! DIG IN!

FACTFILE

WHERE Leave the A861 in Strontian and head north through Anaheilt. Start the climb at the junction, heading left up the hill towards Scotstown.

GRID REF NM 838 664 (OS40)

LENGTH 4650m

HEIGHT GAIN 331m

APPROX CLIMB TIME 18mins

Polloch

SUNART

Scotstown

STRONTIAN   Anaheilt

A861

LOCH SUNART   A884

5km

BEINN NAM BEATHRACH

STRONTIAN, LOCHABER

On my journey north from Mull, lured by a transmitter icon on my map, I was determined to check out this climb. The ascent begins on the A884, following the shores of Loch Sunart – keep an eye out for a small inlet where a stream runs under the road, as this is where the climbing starts. Very slight at first it is only when you bend left, away from the water and towards the hills, that the slope begins to bite. Heading towards the rocky mounds ahead you pass between giant boulders that straddle the road, and here the hard work begins. In a series of prolonged and gruelling straights, and with little protection from the weather, you struggle up to a small stone bridge. As the road bends gently left, the slope seems slightly kinder under the wheel, but it isn't long before you begin another long, strength-sapping straight stretch, all the way to the top.

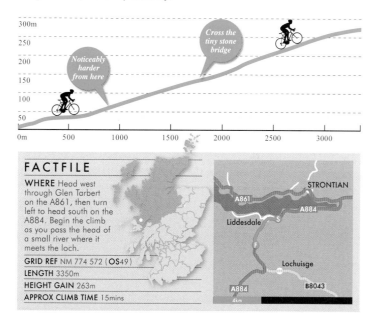

FACTFILE

WHERE Head west through Glen Tarbert on the A861, then turn left to head south on the A884. Begin the climb as you pass the head of a small river where it meets the loch.

GRID REF NM 774 572 (OS49)

LENGTH 3350m

HEIGHT GAIN 263m

APPROX CLIMB TIME 15mins

MCBAIN HILL

DORES, INVERNESS

From the beastly shores of Loch Ness rises this true beauty of a climb, switching back and forth through a slew of tight bends up a heavily forested bank. Packed with testing ramps and devilish corners, this immaculate road cuts its way through such an overwhelming abundance of flora that you might as well be riding through the Chelsea Flower Show. I had initially come to ride the B862 out of Dores, but this road is so much better, all the way from the 90-degree corner at the base. The early slopes are stiff up to the first set of bends – first tight left, then immediately right, both on a relatively mild gradient. You then weave through two more corners, climbing hard up to the second set of hairpins. These ones are tighter, but still not too steep, and they lead into a shallow stretch followed by a dip that allows you to build up the speed you need for the final push to the summit at the junction.

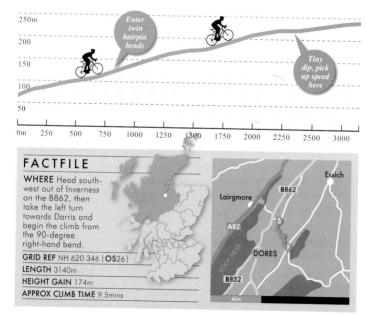

Enter twin hairpin bends

Tiny dip, pick up speed here

250m
200
150
100
50
0m   250   500   750   1000   1250   1500   1750   2000   2250   2500   3000

FACTFILE

WHERE Head south-west out of Inverness on the B862, then take the left turn towards Darris and begin the climb from the 90-degree right-hand bend.

GRID REF NH 620 346 (OS26)

LENGTH 3140m

HEIGHT GAIN 174m

APPROX CLIMB TIME 9.5mins

Essich

B862

Lairgmore

A82

DORES

LOCH NESS

B852

4km

GLEN KYLLACHY

TOMATIN, STRATHDEARN

Travel four kilometres west from Tomatin on a lonely, undulating road and then take a right just before Garbole to reach the base of this perfect little climb. You have two cattle grids to negotiate first and then, bending round a corner, you cross a tiny bridge – this is where the climbing starts. The ascent builds on a consistently increasing gradient until it settles on an almost uniform 7% slope. As you zig-zag through a patchy conifer forest, the surface becomes rough. Make the most of the shelter here because just after halfway you break free from the trees and continue on exposed moorland, set on the same perfect gradient. But there is a surprise in store. The archetypal sting in the tail comes in the shape of a wicked little 20% left-hand bend, just a few hundred metres before the top. Blast through it and keep pushing to the lonely summit.

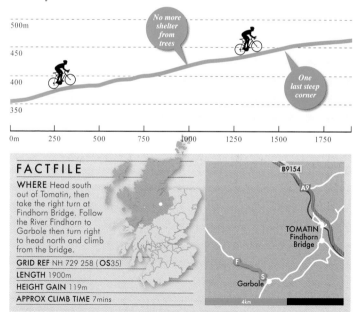

No more shelter from trees

One last steep corner

500m
450
400
350

0m   250   500   750   1000   1250   1500   1750

FACTFILE

WHERE Head south out of Tomatin, then take the right turn at Findhorn Bridge. Follow the River Findhorn to Garbole then turn right to head north and climb from the bridge.

GRID REF NH 729 258 (**OS**35)

LENGTH 1900m

HEIGHT GAIN 119m

APPROX CLIMB TIME 7mins

B9154

A9

TOMATIN
Findhorn
Bridge

F

S

Garbole

4km

CARN AN T-SUIDHE

FORT AUGUSTUS, INVERNESS

This awesome road can be split into four distinct segments, the first of which, climbing out of the congestion of Fort Augustus and up into the woods, is set on a solid 10% slope. This requires a fair amount of grunt to tackle and is followed by a small but significant descent, which on one hand allows a moment of rest, but on the other breaks your climbing rhythm. The road then rises into the third sector, not quite so steep this time, up to the shores of Loch Tarff where, at just over half distance, it levels completely. As the road traces the edge of the small loch stick it in the big ring and power round to the stiff ramp that marks the abrupt end to this kilometre of flat – it is visibly harsh and a proper shock to the legs. Now you are on the final kilometre, stretched out across the moor. After one last tiny drop and a small steep kick, the climb returns to its 7% slog, up to the car park at the brow.

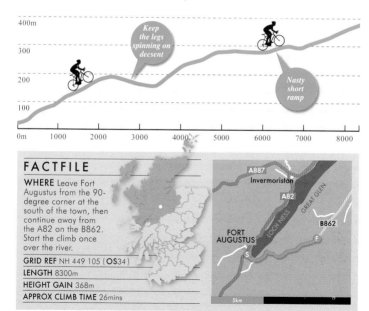

Keep the legs spinning on descent

Nasty short ramp

FACTFILE

WHERE Leave Fort Augustus from the 90-degree corner at the south of the town, then continue away from the A82 on the B862. Start the climb once over the river.

GRID REF NH 449 105 (**OS**34)

LENGTH 8300m

HEIGHT GAIN 368m

APPROX CLIMB TIME 26mins

RATING
6/10

CAIRN GORM

AVIEMORE, CAIRNGORMS

A road to nowhere that resembles some of the world's great mountain climbs, this challenge winds up from the valley to finish high at the ski station by the base for the Cairngorm Funicular Railway. Heading out of Aviemore, the long valley road leads to Glenmore, where the proper climbing begins. Sweeping left then right, it leads up into Glenmore Forest. The road climbs hard, winding on a 7% slope through the conifers, before banking steeply left and levelling out. Further up, following a sharp right-hander, you reach a fork in the road – the beginning of a high altitude one-way system. Bear left, climb, plateau, then follow the road right to climb further, before turning left once again. Here the gradient eases, allowing you to enjoy the spectacular views over Aviemore far below on your way to the finale. At the T-junction bear left and climb to the Alpine summit at the large car park for the railway and Ranger's Base.

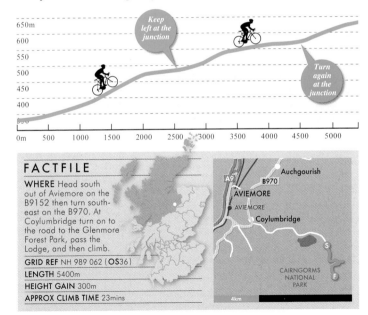

Keep left at the junction

Turn again at the junction

650m
600
550
500
450
400

0m   500   1000   1500   2000   2500   3000   3500   4000   4500   5000

FACTFILE

WHERE Head south out of Aviemore on the B9152 then turn south-east on the B970. At Coylumbridge turn on to the road to the Glenmore Forest Park, pass the Lodge, and then climb.

GRID REF NH 989 062 (OS36)

LENGTH 5400m

HEIGHT GAIN 300m

APPROX CLIMB TIME 23mins

Auchgourish
A9   B970
AVIEMORE
AVIEMORE
Coylumbridge
CAIRNGORMS NATIONAL PARK
4km

RATING

4/10

GLEN COE

BALLACHULISH, LOCHABER

One of the most beautiful and spectacular locations in the whole of Britain, you cannot fail to be in awe of your surroundings as you climb the Pass of Glen Coe. Leave the banks of Loch Leven and head out on the long, flat approach. As you weave right and left, following the river, it is quite a while before you will notice an increase in gradient, but you are climbing. As you trace the banks of the small Loch Achtriochtan the valley opens up, but there is still no serious increase in gradient. It is only when you see the pass heading towards the giant V on the horizon that you feel it bite. The higher you climb, the more the road winds, in a negotiation of the huge outcrops of rock that litter the mountainside – at one point, the road cuts right through one. Passing the numerous viewing points, cascading waterfalls, and even the odd isolated building, you finish this – the most wonderful of roads – on a heavenly plateau at the top.

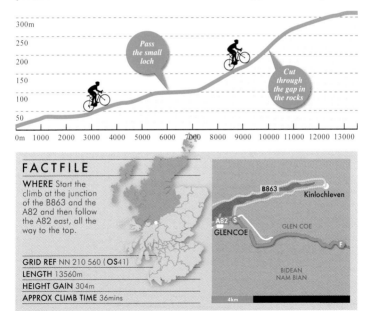

300m
250
200
150
100
50

Pass the small loch

Cut through the gap in the rocks

0m 1000 2000 3000 4000 5000 6000 7000 8000 9000 10000 11000 12000 13000

FACTFILE

WHERE Start the climb at the junction of the B863 and the A82 and then follow the A82 east, all the way to the top.

B863
Kinlochleven
A82 S
GLENCOE
GLEN COE
BIDEAN NAM BIAN
F
4km

GRID REF NN 210 560 (**OS**41)
LENGTH 13560m
HEIGHT GAIN 304m
APPROX CLIMB TIME 36mins

GLEN ETIVE

DALNESS, LOCHABER

I sat deliberating at the top of this climb for quite a while. Do I ride it? Do I include it? There is a fair amount of elevation gain, but it also drops 20 kilometres to the head of Loch Etive… Does it count as a climb? As I looked out along the valley I was all but dragged in, such is the drama and beauty of this road. You will see on the map that I start my measurement from Dalness and not from Gualachulain, as that is where the unbroken climbing begins. For the next ten kilometres the narrow road rises through a pristine glen, following the course of the river and punctuated by a few spikes in gradient and a number of passing places. This upward journey is one of the most wonderful anywhere in Britain, and not too physically demanding as the slopes are largely gradual. As you ride, just relax – spin your gear and soak in the nature. Before you know it you will be back on the A82 at the top.

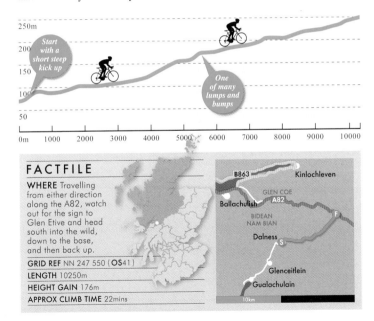

250m
200
150
100
50
0m 1000 2000 3000 4000 5000 6000 7000 8000 9000 10000

Start with a short steep kick up

One of many lumps and bumps

FACTFILE

WHERE Travelling from either direction along the A82, watch out for the sign to Glen Etive and head south into the wild, down to the base, and then back up.

GRID REF NN 247 550 (OS41)

LENGTH 10250m

HEIGHT GAIN 176m

APPROX CLIMB TIME 22mins

B863 — Kinlochleven
GLEN COE — A82
Ballachulish
BIDEAN NAM BIAN
Dalness
Glenceitlein
Gualachulain
10km

EAST
SCOTLAND

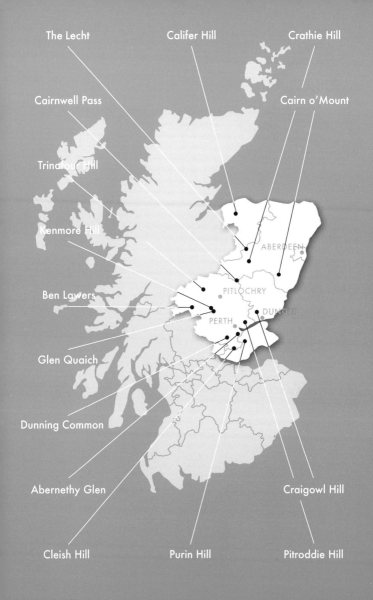

The Lecht

Califer Hill

Crathie Hill

Cairnwell Pass

Cairn o'Mount

Trinafour Hill

Kenmore Hill

ABERDEEN

Ben Lawers

PITLOCHRY

DUNDEE

PERTH

Glen Quaich

Dunning Common

Abernethy Glen

Craigowl Hill

Cleish Hill

Purin Hill

Pitroddie Hill

CALIFER HILL

CALIFER, MORAY

It is not hilly in these parts – far from it – but I was determined to find a climb, and find one I did. To make the most of the ascent I have measured it all the way from the B9010 just south of Forres, but to begin with you will hardly notice you are climbing. Crossing the first of two junctions you soon reach a left-hand kink and it is here that the climb begins to rise harshly, just past the entrance to New Forres Quarry. Bending gradually right, following the edge of the wood, you continue to climb up to the second junction, from where you will catch sight of the rest of your challenge. Following a brief levelling the gradient rapidly picks up and the slope is a consistent test as you weave up and away from the flat plains below. After passing through Califer, climbing all the way, you will reach two distinct left-hand bends and then finally the brow dividing the trees – the end to a surprisingly tough climb.

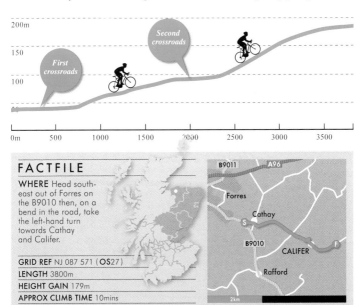

FACTFILE

WHERE Head south-east out of Forres on the B9010 then, on a bend in the road, take the left-hand turn towards Cathay and Califer.

GRID REF NJ 087 571 (OS27)

LENGTH 3800m

HEIGHT GAIN 179m

APPROX CLIMB TIME 10mins

RATING
10/10

THE LECHT

A true monster of a climb through the heart of the Cairngorms National Park, the road up to the Lecht Ski Centre is a simply stunning ride. You start your ascent from the beautiful Corgarff Castle and straight away you hit 20% slopes – rough, relentlessly steep and twisting a little. Pass through the large orange gates used to close the road in winter – proof, if you hadn't twigged already, that you are heading into serious country. After an age on the steep opening gradient the road banks right to plateau before a brief downhill. What comes next will take your breath away. There in front of you, painted on to the side of the mountain and resembling a giant flight of stairs, lies the rest of the climb. A short flat section ramps up hard, then almost levels before ramping up hard again. Eventually you will bend round to the left and the battered, rugged road levels for good. In front of you is the Alpine-style ski station – just awesome.

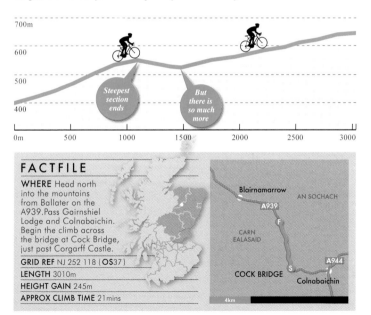

Steepest section ends

But there is so much more

FACTFILE

WHERE Head north into the mountains from Ballater on the A939. Pass Gairnshiel Lodge and Colnabaichin. Begin the climb across the bridge at Cock Bridge, just past Corgarff Castle.

GRID REF NJ 252 118 (**OS**37)

LENGTH 3010m

HEIGHT GAIN 245m

APPROX CLIMB TIME 21mins

RATING
6/10

CRATHIE HILL

CRATHIE, ABERDEENSHIRE

Crathie Hill makes for an excellent diversion from the main road if you are travelling north through the Cairngorms National Park. Start the climb from the A93 across the road from Balmoral Castle and begin to weave through the woods past the occasional farm building. Following a prolonged right turn the slope recedes to cross a small stone bridge before bending left into more woods. As the road straightens you see the slope gradually rise up in front of you, bisecting the trees – the mere sight of this increase in pitch will have you changing down. Once you are free of the woods the scenery opens up to reveal glorious moorland and empty rolling hills. Now on an easier pitch, you can take a few moments to appreciate your surroundings before entering the final section. After a slight bend left the road kicks up to a false summit, and then it's another slightly harder stretch to the true top alongside a lone cairn.

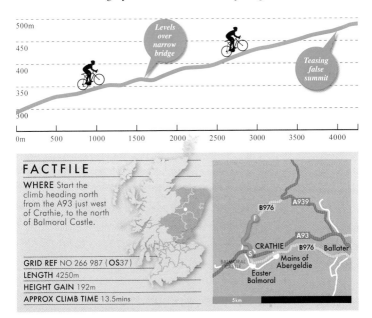

FACTFILE

WHERE Start the climb heading north from the A93 just west of Crathie, to the north of Balmoral Castle.

GRID REF NO 266 987 (OS37)

LENGTH 4250m

HEIGHT GAIN 192m

APPROX CLIMB TIME 13.5mins

RATING 7/10

CAIRN O'MOUNT

FETTERCAIRN, ABERDEENSHIRE

A couple of miles north of Fettercairn lies the small and welcoming outpost of the Clatterin' Brig Tea Room. Rising sharply from the base of its steep driveway, the B974 heads into the mountains to summit at Cairn o'Mount. Beginning hard, at 16%, the reasonably wide road bends left then heads straight up. The gradient eases only slightly on the ascent to a ruined building on your left, its remaining stones just about clinging to the hillside. Bending right past the ruins the gradient eases for some time and the long middle section runs along a rough but well-surfaced road marked with snow poles. Although far more gentle than the start, it is not quite easy enough for you to recover in time for the 14% top section ahead. Easing right, then turning hard left before one last hard right, you are into the final push. Finish alongside a small car park as the road disappears down the other side into Glen Dye.

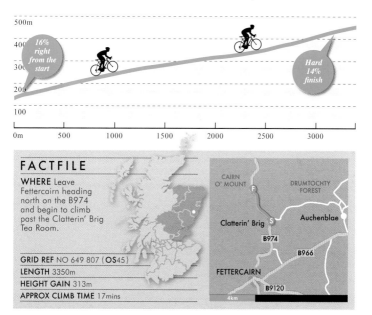

FACTFILE

WHERE Leave Fettercairn heading north on the B974 and begin to climb past the Clatterin' Brig Tea Room.

GRID REF NO 649 807 (**OS**45)	
LENGTH 3350m	
HEIGHT GAIN 313m	
APPROX CLIMB TIME 17mins	

CAIRNWELL PASS

SPITTAL OF GLENSHEE, PERTH AND KINROSS

The Cairnwell Pass is a giant arc of a climb that guides you deep into the Cairngorms National Park. As the principle route north for miles around the road is often busy, but it is plenty wide enough for bicycles. Ride past the Spittal of Glenshee, the last settlement for some distance, and head through the beautiful valley approaching the climb. Although you are gradually gaining altitude the climbing doesn't truly begin until the road turns right. Here it begins its majestic sweep up into the mountains at 12% from start to finish. You pass 'no stopping' signs on either side of the road, which gently banks left as the stiff gradient pulls you out of the valley. Now comes the long and straight stretch of the climb, where the gutter is punctuated with deep-set iron grilles. Bending slightly left towards the brow you pass Devil's Elbow on your right and roll over the top, past the Glenshee Ski Centre and into the majestic Cairngorms.

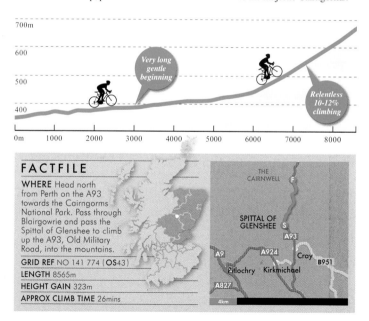

Very long gentle beginning

Relentless 10-12% climbing

FACTFILE

WHERE Head north from Perth on the A93 towards the Cairngorms National Park. Pass through Blairgowrie and pass the Spittal of Glenshee to climb up the A93, Old Military Road, into the mountains.

GRID REF NO 141 774 (**OS**43)

LENGTH 8565m

HEIGHT GAIN 323m

APPROX CLIMB TIME 26mins

RATING
9/10

CRAIGOWL HILL

TEALING, ANGUS

The multitude of aerials that sit on top of Craigowl Hill can be seen for miles around and, like the mythical Greek Sirens, they lure riders in before destroying their legs on the vicious slopes. Begin your ascent from the crossroads at the base and rise past various farmhouses to where the road bends left. As you pick your way up the early slopes the task that awaits you comes into view, and it is enough to send a shiver down the spine. Climbing in a direct line, without an inch of deviation, the narrow and debris-strewn road heads straight up the hillside. It appears, and indeed is, a formidable stretch of tarmac, which at its most punishing hits 20%. Square ahead stand the collection of transmitters, but to reach them you must first circumnavigate the top of the mound. Riding in a giant circle, on a thankfully kinder gradient, you spiral in on the summit to finish with a final hard ramp up to the solitude of the lone peak.

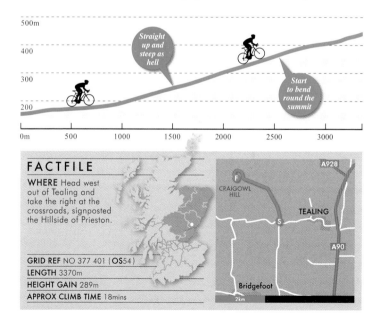

FACTFILE

WHERE Head west out of Tealing and take the right at the crossroads, signposted the Hillside of Prieston.

GRID REF NO 377 401 (OS54)

LENGTH 3370m

HEIGHT GAIN 289m

APPROX CLIMB TIME 18mins

PITRODDIE HILL

PITRODDIE, PERTH AND KINROSS

Of the many climbs that criss-cross the Braes of the Carse I decided to ride three, then pick one to include in the book. I first tackled the road north out of Glendoick, then the slightly longer ascent from Kilspindie, before riding this climb sandwiched between them. The slightly longer, twisting ascent out of Kilspindie almost got the nod, but in the end I decided this was the greater challenge. The narrow road starts by weaving through high hedgerows, climbing a small bump, and then dropping down past some farmhouses. From here you climb up the valley on a gradient well into double figures. With Pole Hill over your right shoulder you head left to continue on a 10% average for almost a kilometre. Straight to begin with, it is a real slog to the right-hand bend where you line up to the summit that lies just past the small clump of trees on the horizon.

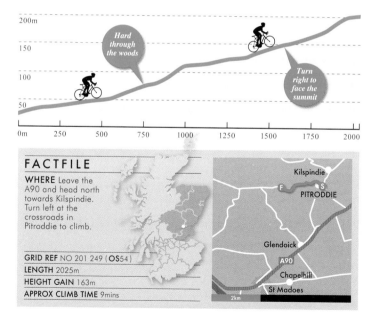

Hard through the woods

Turn right to face the summit

FACTFILE

WHERE Leave the A90 and head north towards Kilspindie. Turn left at the crossroads in Pitroddie to climb.

GRID REF NO 201 249 (**OS54**)

LENGTH 2025m

HEIGHT GAIN 163m

APPROX CLIMB TIME 9mins

Kilspindie

PITRODDIE

Glendoick

A90

Chapelhill

St Madoes

ABERNETHY GLEN

ABERNETHY, PERTH AND KINROSS

Running parallel to – and rising gently away from – the A913, this is a surprisingly
tough climb. With the ridge looming over your right shoulder it isn't long before
you encounter signs warning of a narrow twisting road ahead. As you get stuck in to
the long, straight path through Glenfoot, you know you are in the right place. Upon
entering the woods the weaving begins, first heading right, where the pitch of the road
creeps into the double figures and demands a couple of gear changes. Significantly
more effort is needed through the next right and left bends between the hedgerows.
Thankfully the tougher gradients don't hang around for long and soon you hit the
significant downhill that bisects the climbing. Now on a shallow slope you head south
past clumps of forest and rolling, grassy fields to reach the sharp kick to the summit,
which sits at a right-hand bend adjacent to a parking place on your left.

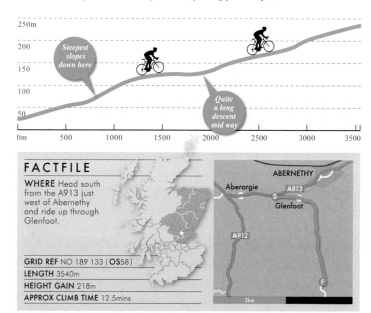

FACTFILE

WHERE Head south
from the A913 just
west of Abernethy
and ride up through
Glenfoot.

GRID REF NO 189 133 (**OS**58)

LENGTH 3540m

HEIGHT GAIN 218m

APPROX CLIMB TIME 12.5mins

DUNNING COMMON

DUNNING, PERTH AND KINROSS

Long for this part of Scotland (over five kilometres) but never too steep, the road up to the summit of Dunning Common is packed with turns and glorious views. Leave Dunning on Muckhart Street and head due south towards the rolling hills ahead. It is a while before the gradient begins to bite, and when it does it is more toothless baby than Great White shark. There are a couple of stiffer patches along its course that may force a change of gear, but for the most part the slope is a civilised 5%. Framed by high hedgerows from bottom to top, the road is also well protected from the wind, and to help you even further, there is a slight levelling ahead of the last 1,500 metres. Make sure to look back a couple of times to appreciate the view while pressing forward on your search for the summit, which lies just past the large house on the hillside.

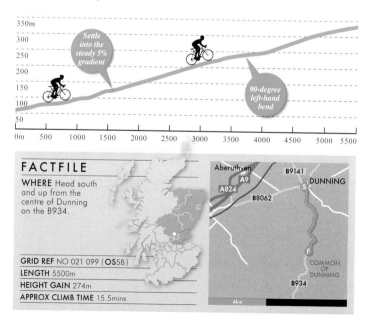

Settle into the steady 5% gradient

90-degree left-hand bend

FACTFILE

WHERE Head south and up from the centre of Dunning on the B934.

GRID REF NO 021 099 (**OS**58)

LENGTH 5500m

HEIGHT GAIN 274m

APPROX CLIMB TIME 15.5mins

RATING
5/10

CLEISH HILL

CLEISH, PERTH AND KINROSS

Another of Fife's many gems, Cleish Hill stands proud above the surrounding farmland and offers a substantial test for all who dare to take up its challenge. After a sign warning of tight bends for the next three miles the slope gradually begins to build, negotiating a scattering of farmhouses and heading for the rocky outcrop ahead. With rolling grassland to your left and woodland on your right, you follow an increasingly stiff slope up to the first tight bend. Heading left the slope ramps up some more, demanding a little more graft and revealing stunning views out over Loch Leven. Next, bending gradually right, there is a slight easing before a sharp increase to a false summit that, although not the top, ushers in the final part of the climb. Continually turning right and on an ever-decreasing pitch, you roll on through the rough grassland to the top, which lies between a pair of metal gates.

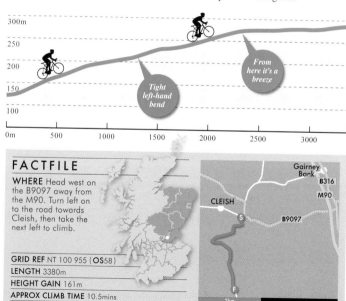

Tight left-hand bend

From here it's a breeze

FACTFILE

WHERE Head west on the B9097 away from the M90. Turn left on to the road towards Cleish, then take the next left to climb.

GRID REF NT 100 955 (**OS**58)

LENGTH 3380m

HEIGHT GAIN 161m

APPROX CLIMB TIME 10.5mins

PURIN HILL

FALKLAND, FIFE

Be warned: if you have come here to try and beat the best time for this climb, you better be fit. This climb is used for racing, and the evidence is quite literally all over it. Painted on to the well-maintained surface at intervals from the halfway point to the summit are a series of lines and measurements. Acting as carrots to chase, or maybe mental hurdles to cross, they count up (not down) all the way to the finish line. Start from the A90 and twist up on a stiff but changeable gradient though the woods. As you exit the trees there is a kink right and then left, where the slope eases before picking up to a 90-degree right-hand bend. After this you enter two sections of straight climbing and the pitch becomes a challenge. The first section is short, while the second inches close to a kilometre. A series of miniscule relaxations of the gradient punctuate the arduous slog, but it is the numbers gliding under your wheels that will eventually pull you to the top.

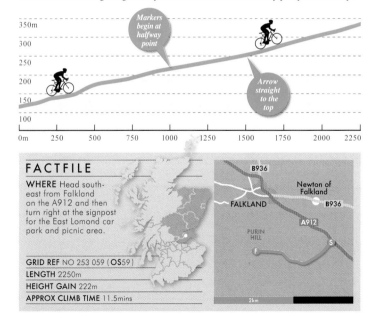

Markers begin at halfway point

Arrow straight to the top

| 350m |
| 300 |
| 250 |
| 200 |
| 150 |
| 100 |

| 0m | 250 | 500 | 750 | 1000 | 1250 | 1500 | 1750 | 2000 | 2250 |

FACTFILE

WHERE Head south-east from Falkland on the A912 and then turn right at the signpost for the East Lomond car park and picnic area.

| **GRID REF** NO 253 059 (**OS**59) |
| **LENGTH** 2250m |
| **HEIGHT GAIN** 222m |
| **APPROX CLIMB TIME** 11.5mins |

B936

Newton of Falkland

FALKLAND   B936

A912

PURIN HILL

F

S

2km

TRINAFOUR HILL

TRINAFOUR, PERTH AND KINROSS

If I followed up every suggestion I received to go and check out climbs I would never be off my bike. But so persistent was one reader on the merits of this road that I was compelled to investigate it further, and I am so glad I did. Ramping up hard from the get-go you rise through a small wood on a gradient well over 10%. After breaking free from the trees you turn right, where the slope backs off a touch up to the first hairpin. Banking steep left you head back on yourself, then ride up to two more beautiful bends. The first is classically Alpine, smooth and wide, a 180-degree curve that leads almost directly into the next, a slightly steeper corner. Once through these thrilling turns there is a long push to the top (marked by a clump of trees) across beautiful open land. You have one more short, stiff stretch to face after this, but generally the slope fades on the approach to the summit.

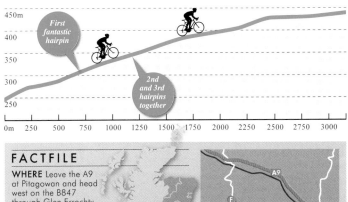

FACTFILE

WHERE Leave the A9 at Pitagowan and head west on the B847 through Glen Errochty. At Trinafour turn off the main road into the village and begin the climb when the road bends right.

GRID REF NN 728 669 (OS42)

LENGTH 3150m

HEIGHT GAIN 196m

APPROX CLIMB TIME 11mins

BEN LAWERS

BRIDGE OF BALGIE, PERTH AND KINROSS

Here we have a long, long climb on multiple surfaces with varying gradients – none too steep, but plenty of them. Start from the entrance to the Meggernie Outdoor Centre and rise up to cross the first cattle grid. The early slopes are gentle, winding this way and that towards a small wooded area where the tarmac changes colour and the gradient eases. Leaving the trees behind you cross a second cattle grid, after which the slope ramps up. As you twist and snake your way up each corner reveals an ever grander view of the valley below. You will never be overwhelmed by this climb, as the distance between corners is always short, allowing you to refresh your mind and tackle each stretch as a separate task. As an added bonus, the closer you get to the top, the easier it is to climb. You can pick up some real speed to finish at the brow just shy of a small blue sign next to a pile of stones.

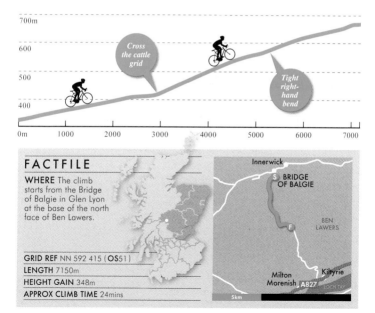

FACTFILE

WHERE The climb starts from the Bridge of Balgie in Glen Lyon at the base of the north face of Ben Lawers.

GRID REF NN 592 415 (OS51)
LENGTH 7150m
HEIGHT GAIN 348m
APPROX CLIMB TIME 24mins

KENMORE HILL

KENMORE, PERTH AND KINROSS

This climb has everything. It is as savage as it is beautiful, and as demanding as it is rewarding, which is why, even though I have already included the southern ascent of this hill (see page 84), I just had to include it. The climb begins with a bang, right from the point where you leave the A827 and head up the 10-15% slopes, punctuated with wicked 20% corners, that twist through the thick forest. If these brutal lower slopes break you then you will be glad of the small amount of level terrain that follows them, which allows you to gather yourself before the next hard stretch that leads to the easier climbing further up. After a right-hand turn in front of a lone house you hit a 15% slope that takes you first left and then right to a merciful easing of the gradient. There is little protection from the elements on the open land up here, so you will have to battle the wind past the tiny loch. Keep the pressure on until you are sure you can climb no more.

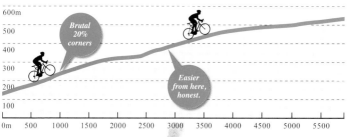

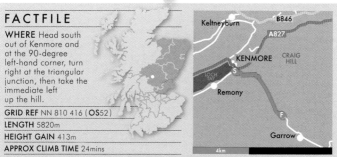

FACTFILE

WHERE Head south out of Kenmore and at the 90-degree left-hand corner, turn right at the triangular junction, then take the immediate left up the hill.

GRID REF NN 810 416 (OS52)

LENGTH 5820m

HEIGHT GAIN 413m

APPROX CLIMB TIME 24mins

RATING
7/10

GLEN QUAICH

GARROW, PERTH AND KINROSS

As you will see, I have included both sides of this pass in the book as they are both totally awesome, yet totally different in character. The south side casts its spell as you approach through the glen – up ahead you will see a dark line rising over the hillside. At first glance it resembles a stone wall, but it is too wide... It couldn't be the climb, surely not – that would be insane! But as you get closer, it slowly starts to dawn on you that it is in fact the road, and your heart begins to thump. Starting from the small bridge at its base it is steep straight away and the surface is just wonderful, as smooth as rolled icing. The slope eases past some trees on your left and then it is hard up to the first cattle grid. It backs off a little again on the approach to the right-left switchbacks. Past these it is steep all the way to the second cattle grid, where there is a final lull in the action before one last vicious ramp that takes you to the summit.

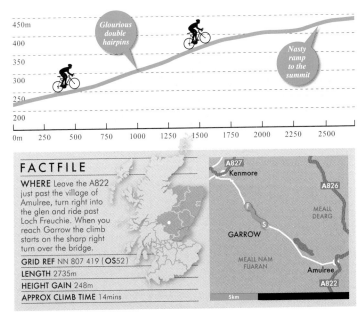

Glourious double hairpins

Nasty ramp to the summit

FACTFILE

WHERE Leave the A822 just past the village of Amulree, turn right into the glen and ride past Loch Freuchie. When you reach Garrow the climb starts on the sharp right turn over the bridge.

GRID REF NN 807 419 (**OS**52)

LENGTH 2735m

HEIGHT GAIN 248m

APPROX CLIMB TIME 14mins

WEST
SCOTLAND

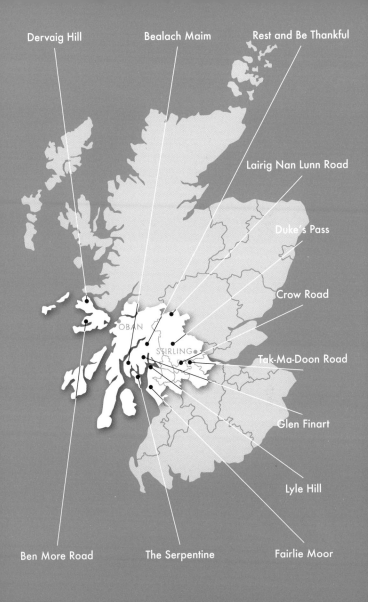

Dervaig Hill

Bealach Maim

Rest and Be Thankful

Lairig Nan Lunn Road

Duke's Pass

Crow Road

OBAN

STIRLING

Tak-Ma-Doon Road

Glen Finart

Lyle Hill

Ben More Road

The Serpentine

Fairlie Moor

LAIRIG NAN LUNN ROAD

KENKNOCK, STIRLING

This climb is so far off the beaten track that the beaten track is a distant memory once you eventually reach the base. Built to access the hydroelectric plant, the road features two gates and is unsealed in places (so if like me you turn up on 23mm slick tyres, you may experience a little wheel spin). You reach the first of the two kissing gates almost right away, but once you have passed through it you can begin your battle against the testing gradient and crumbling surface. It is always steep and in places little more than a gravel track, but if you study the path ahead you will be able to pick a reasonably intact line to ride. I spent most of my time in the saddle to aid traction on the rougher parts, but had to ride standing up though the steep tight corners. This road is wild, rugged, lonely and exposed the whole way up, although after the second gate and over the top the surface is much better.

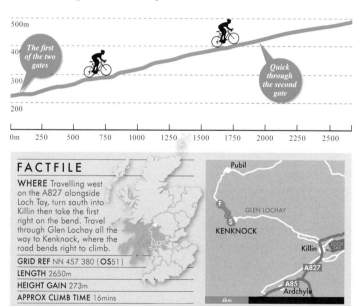

500m

400 — **The first of the two gates**

300 — **Quick through the second gate**

200

0m   250   500   750   1000   1250   1500   1750   2000   2250   2500

FACTFILE

WHERE Travelling west on the A827 alongside Loch Tay, turn south into Killin then take the first right on the bend. Travel through Glen Lochay all the way to Kenknock, where the road bends right to climb.

GRID REF NN 457 380 (**OS**51)

LENGTH 2650m

HEIGHT GAIN 273m

APPROX CLIMB TIME 16mins

Pubil

GLEN LOCHAY

KENKNOCK

Killin

A827

A85
Ardchyle

4km

DUKE'S PASS

ABERFOYLE, STIRLING

Rising through the Achray Forest into the heart of the beautiful Trossachs National Park, this road serves up its climbing in multiple stages. Leave Aberfoyle as the A821 bends right on to Hillside, ride up through the houses, and then follow the road left to the entrance of David Marshall Lodge. The slope eases into a majestic right-hand bend that leads immediately into a left-hander, where the climbing picks up. Up to the next tight corners you have stunning views on your right, before the road heads up and away from them towards the plateau at the Duke's Pass sign. Here you could let your legs recover, or wind it up through the rocky landscape making its way to the right to reach the last stretch of climbing. This last long section isn't too tough, and you roll to a finish just past the entrance to the Achray Forest Drive. Now you can enjoy the brilliant descent to Loch Achray.

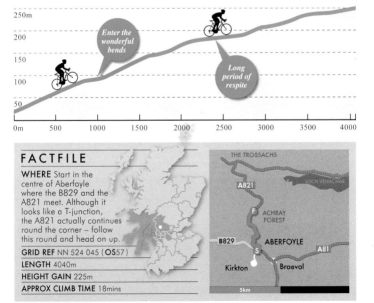

Enter the wonderful bends

Long period of respite

FACTFILE

WHERE Start in the centre of Aberfoyle where the B829 and the A821 meet. Although it looks like a T-junction, the A821 actually continues round the corner – follow this round and head on up.

GRID REF NN 524 045 (**OS**57)

LENGTH 4040m

HEIGHT GAIN 225m

APPROX CLIMB TIME 18mins

CROW ROAD

LENNOXTOWN, EAST DUNBARTONSHIRE

Rising out of Lennoxtown and traversing the Campsie Fells north of Glasgow is the B822, or Crow Road. It is relatively easy at first, but as you head out of town it ramps up to 10%, if not steeper – the gradient eases back a touch after this, but only slightly. Now you have the long slog up the side of the Fells. The road, a single great scar on the 45-degree grassy banks, gradually makes its way skyward. What few trees there are on the lower slopes are soon replaced by a single metal barrier on your left, which shields you from the drop but also hems you in. It is a relief to reach the 90-degree right-hand turn where the road opens up a little. A gentle stretch takes you past the car park but now you are into the hard part. Give it all you've got because once up this short rise it is a doddle to the top. If the wind is blowing in the right direction, stick it in the big ring and pick up speed to power the rest of the way to the finish.

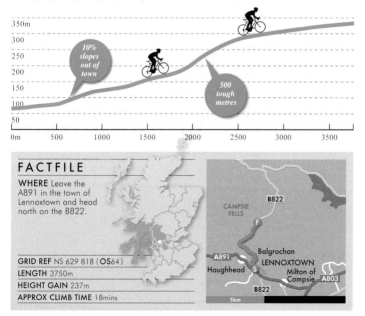

10% slopes out of town

500 tough metres

FACTFILE

WHERE Leave the A891 in the town of Lennoxtown and head north on the B822.

GRID REF NS 629 818 (OS64)

LENGTH 3750m

HEIGHT GAIN 237m

APPROX CLIMB TIME 18mins

CAMPSIE FELLS

B822

Balgrochan

A891   LENNOXTOWN

Haughhead   Milton of Campsie

A803

B822

5km

RATING
7/10

TAK-MA-DOON ROAD

KILSYTH, NORTH LANARKSHIRE

With more twists and false endings than a cheap crime novel, this testing climb up over the Kilsyth Hills will keep you guessing all the way to the top. Branching off Stirling Road in Kilsyth, the road heads north out of town and quickly bends right into a hard 10% push through the houses. After a slight leveling it climbs up once more, to meet a distinct brow followed by a tiny descent. Next you head left into the easiest part of the ascent. The pitch soon increases again, as the road begins to writhe across a landscape framed by crumbling stone walls up to a pronounced brow. The summit? Alas, no – you're not there yet. Twist left, drop down, climb hard back up, and then repeat a similar sequence after this before embarking on the push to the true summit. It is a real grind up this seemingly endless hillside, the road kinking incrementally left as you creep and grovel your way to the welcome relief of the viewpoint at its peak.

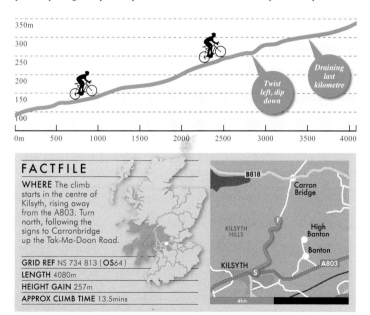

FACTFILE

WHERE The climb starts in the centre of Kilsyth, rising away from the A803. Turn north, following the signs to Carronbridge up the Tak-Ma-Doon Road.

GRID REF NS 734 813 (**OS**64)

LENGTH 4080m

HEIGHT GAIN 257m

APPROX CLIMB TIME 13.5mins

REST AND BE THANKFUL

CAIRNDOW, ARGYLL AND BUTE

In 1753, a stone was placed at the top of this climb by soldiers who built the first road over the pass, bearing the words 'Rest and Be Thankful'. The original stone is long gone and a car park now sits in its place, at the point where the A83 meets the B828. It is a tough climb up the A83 from either direction, but the harder, quieter and wilder climb is up the B-road from Hell's Glen. Pedalling up the immaculate single-track road you will find the fluctuating gradient isn't too tough to begin with as frequent level stretches offer some respite. As the forest opens up, the ascent eases further, but once you are over a small stone bridge it is solid climbing until the end. Freshly re-surfaced, the road follows the river and throws in a couple of 16% corners: left, then very steep right. Leaving the forest and the hardest climbing behind you, roll along to the radio mast at the top, then descend to rest, and be thankful.

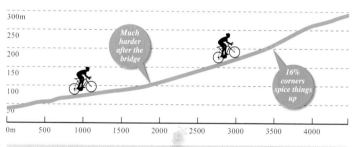

Much harder after the bridge

16% corners spice things up

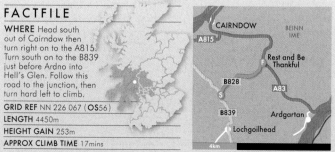

FACTFILE

WHERE Head south out of Cairndow then turn right on to the A815. Turn south on to the B839 just before Ardno into Hell's Glen. Follow this road to the junction, then turn hard left to climb.

GRID REF NN 226 067 (**OS56**)

LENGTH 4450m

HEIGHT GAIN 253m

APPROX CLIMB TIME 17mins

RATING
6/10

GLEN FINART

BARNACABBER, ARGYLL AND BUTE

You might expect a road through a glen to be flat but this is Scotland, and this glen has a serious climb in it. Ride out of Ardentinny, through Barnacabber, and then begin to climb once you reach the second of two large totem-like poles on your left. Gentle at first, things start to get interesting once you pass some more poles and a faded 1-in-5 sign. After crossing a bridge you are climbing hard, not quite at 1-in-5 yet, but close. Sweeping left into a long bend, follow the road as it arcs right and then take a breather on a slight easing. It is now that you will spot your task up ahead, etched into the landscape. You first turn right and then you are on to a steep straight stretch before a very steep left-hand turn (more like 1-in-4) that leads to a pronounced crest in the road – unfortunately, it is not the top. You first have to dip down round a protruding rock face and tackle one more upward stretch to finish at a passing place on the brow.

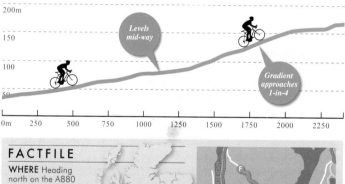

Levels mid-way

Gradient approaches 1-in-4

FACTFILE

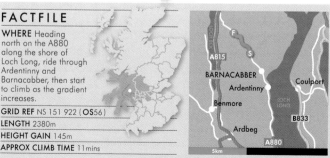

WHERE Heading north on the A880 along the shore of Loch Long, ride through Ardentinny and Barnacabber, then start to climb as the gradient increases.

GRID REF NS 151 922 (**OS**56)

LENGTH 2380m

HEIGHT GAIN 145m

APPROX CLIMB TIME 11mins

BEALACH MAIM

CLACHAN OF GLENDARUEL, ARGYLL AND BUTE

A good way to sum up this climb would be to say the eastern face is Cinderella and the western face – documented here – is one (if not both) of the ugly sisters. Rough and relentless, its surface is broken and overgrown with grass, and its corners are brutal. Start from the small bridge, ride up to and past some farm buildings and then, as the rippled topping turns a distinctive red colour, you will feel the gradient begin to bite. The road is steep and gets steeper still, up to almost 20%, as it approaches what may be Scotland's steepest corner. It is 30% at the apex, and once you have made it through things do not get any easier. The road, now characterised by a foot of grass growing on the crown, is wild in every sense. Plough on, through bend after bend, on to the summit – there are a few let-ups in the rough terrain, but nothing significant until the surface finally improves and you come to a halt. Ugly doesn't even come close.

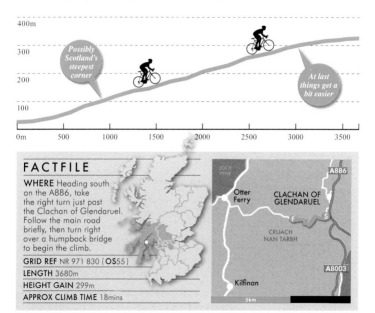

Possibly Scotland's steepest corner

At last things get a bit easier

FACTFILE

WHERE Heading south on the A886, take the right turn just past the Clachan of Glendaruel. Follow the main road briefly, then turn right over a humpback bridge to begin the climb.

GRID REF NR 971 830 (**OS**55)

LENGTH 3680m

HEIGHT GAIN 299m

APPROX CLIMB TIME 18mins

RATING
4/10

THE SERPENTINE

ROTHESAY, ISLE OF BUTE

When I first saw this climb featured in the pages of *Cycling Weekly*, my jaw literally dropped and hit the desk – how had this passed under my radar?! As soon as was physically possible I planned a trip north, caught the ferry across to Bute, and raced to its base. On the approach up Castle Road you see the spectacular concertina of hairpins above you and feel a surge of adrenaline. First you twist left, then right, before you negotiate Mount Pleasant Road to tackle The Serpentine. With 14 tight corners from base to summit it is enough to send you dizzy – left, right, left you twist, all the while looking for the best line in and out of each apex. Slightly ahead of the houses at the top the frequency of the corners decreases, as does the pitch of the slope, and if you have ridden it full gas all the way, the last straight to the T-junction will really make the legs burn. A truly magnificent road.

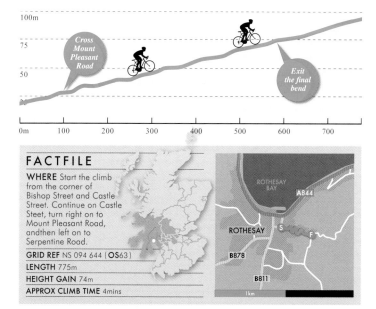

Cross Mount Pleasant Road

Exit the final bend

FACTFILE

WHERE Start the climb from the corner of Bishop Street and Castle Street. Continue on Castle Steet, turn right on to Mount Pleasant Road, andthen left on to Serpentine Road.

GRID REF NS 094 644 (**OS**63)

LENGTH 775m

HEIGHT GAIN 74m

APPROX CLIMB TIME 4mins

ROTHESAY BAY
A844
ROTHESAY
S
F
B878
B811
1km

LYLE HILL

GREENOCK, INVERCLYDE

This demanding road is the second of two urban climbs in the book, and it is often used for hill climb races by local cycling clubs such as Inverclyde Velo. You are treated to a few metres of flat under the rail bridge at the start, and then the road bends right and ramps up. Almost immediately you bend back on yourself through a left-hand hairpin, before heading right straight away to face a right-hand hairpin. It is steep between the bends and even steeper round them, the second surfaced with a distinctively pale and abrasive topping. Out of the corner the gradient remains stiff and you begin a long arc round to the left, climbing past a row of houses on your right. The solid 10% slope really starts to bite as you reach a convoluted junction, where you sweep left to line up for the top. Ahead you will see the giant, part cross, part anchor war memorial – aim for this, now on an easier slope, and keep riding to the parking place at the lookout point.

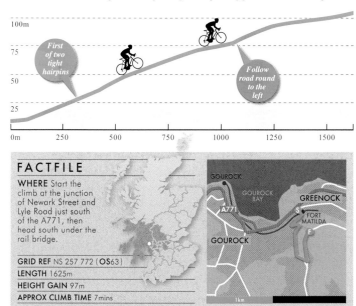

FACTFILE

WHERE Start the climb at the junction of Newark Street and Lyle Road just south of the A771, then head south under the rail bridge.

GRID REF NS 257 772 (OS63)
LENGTH 1625m
HEIGHT GAIN 97m
APPROX CLIMB TIME 7mins

RATING

7/10

FAIRLIE MOOR

FAIRLIE, NORTH AYRSHIRE

I was out before breakfast to ride this climb and, as you can see in the photo opposite, it was a stunning morning offering breathtaking views out over Bute. To climb it, leave the A78, pass under the rail bridge, and plunge briefly into darkness under a thick canopy of trees. Immediately the gradient is nasty, touching 15%, and the road continues to rise sharply as it bends left. Ahead there are numerous clumps of conifers and once you reach them the slope relaxes. Next you cross a cattle grid and ahead see a brow on the horizon of the now open moor. As you close in on it you realise this isn't the top, and another summit reveals itself a few hundred metres further on. But this isn't the end either – a third pronounced brow soon appears. Following a small dip the climbing is a little tougher, but this time you do arrive at the summit, where you must turn round to survey the view out over the islands below.

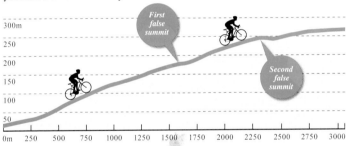

First false summit

Second false summit

300m
250
200
150
100
50
0m   250   500   750   1000   1250   1500   1750   2000   2250   2500   2750   3000

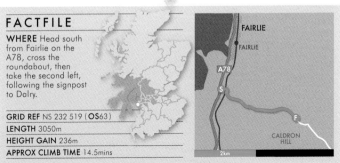

FACTFILE

WHERE Head south from Fairlie on the A78, cross the roundabout, then take the second left, following the signpost to Dalry.

GRID REF NS 232 519 (**OS63**)

LENGTH 3050m

HEIGHT GAIN 236m

APPROX CLIMB TIME 14.5mins

FAIRLIE

FAIRLIE

A78

S

F

CALDRON HILL

2km

DERVAIG HILL

DERVAIG, ISLE OF MULL

I encountered a little bit of rain on my visit to Mull, but in some ways I think I would have been disappointed if I hadn't. Anyway, hostile weather really brings this island to life. Begin this climb from the small bridge at the head of Loch a' Chumhainn and make your way through the village of Dervaig, following the signs to Tobermory. The road begins to twist and the gradient rapidly increases, forcing you instinctively from your saddle. After a few hundred metres of around 12% the slope eases back but continues to snake this way and that, past the houses dotted along its path. The pitch begins to increase again on the approach to a tight hairpin bend, but then eases off again slightly before the push to the top. Here lie the final collection of corners, set in battered and rugged grassland. Let the transmitter mast on the horizon guide you through their glorious, sweeping curves.

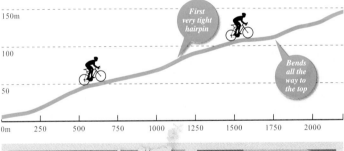

First very tight hairpin

Bends all the way to the top

150m

100

50

0m   250   500   750   1000   1250   1500   1750   2000

FACTFILE

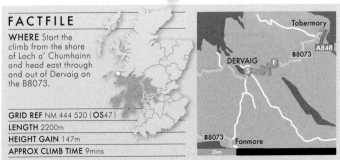

WHERE Start the climb from the shore of Loch a' Chumhainn and head east through and out of Dervaig on the B8073.

GRID REF NM 444 520 (**OS47**)

LENGTH 2200m

HEIGHT GAIN 147m

APPROX CLIMB TIME 9mins

BEN MORE ROAD

BALNAHARD, ISLE OF MULL

In the shadow of Ben More, crossing the Ardmeanach Peninsula on the Isle of Mull, this climb rears up from the waves crashing on the weather-beaten rocky shore and heads inland. Travelling due south, the tiny road clings to the edge of the island and rises gently towards a 90-degree left-hand bend. After this the slope picks up and ahead you see the road wind round the hills and disappear out of sight. On the approach to a solitary white cottage on a slight bend you can enjoy a relatively gentle gradient, before taking a look over your right shoulder. Framed by towering cliffs, the views out to sea are simply outstanding. Once past the lone house there is a spike in the gradient that continues to become more pronounced on the lead up to the brow. Up over this mini peak the slope eases and the final kilometre of climbing between steep rocky banks either side is a breeze.

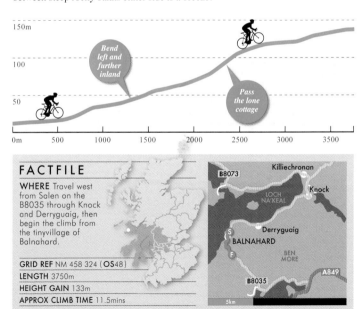

150m

100

50

0m   500   1000   1500   2000   2500   3000   3500

Bend left and further inland

Pass the lone cottage

FACTFILE

WHERE Travel west from Salen on the B8035 through Knock and Derryguaig, then begin the climb from the tinyvillage of Balnahard.

GRID REF NM 458 324 (OS48)

LENGTH 3750m

HEIGHT GAIN 133m

APPROX CLIMB TIME 11.5mins

Killiechronan
B8073
Knock
LOCH NA'KEAL
Derryguaig
BALNAHARD
BEN MORE
A849
B8035
5km

SOUTHERN
SCOTLAND

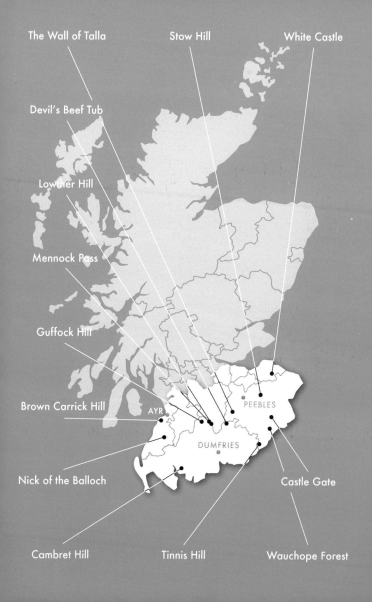

The Wall of Talla

Stow Hill

White Castle

Devil's Beef Tub

Lowther Hill

Mennock Pass

Guffock Hill

Brown Carrick Hill

AYR

PEEBLES

DUMFRIES

Nick of the Balloch

Castle Gate

Cambret Hill

Tinnis Hill

Wauchope Forest

WHITE CASTLE

GARVALD, EAST LOTHIAN

Taking its name from the remains of the Iron Age hill fort towards its summit, this climb had me doubting its credentials at the start, but then it surprised me with a truly stupendous finale. Once out of Garvald the road immediately bends left, and soon after right. It is hard work for the first kilometre, before the gradient eases and levels on the approach to a slight descent. After this the slope kicks up sharply once more, before settling down to trundle between farmhouses and the occasional tree. At this point on my ride I was beginning to feel disheartened, but then, through the last of the trees, I caught a glimpse of my challenge ahead. Marked by twisting barriers, glinting in the sun, the ferocious finale wriggled its way over the hillside. Increasingly tough as you make your way up, with both a number of curves and a brace of vicious ramps, it is both a serious challenge and an utter joy.

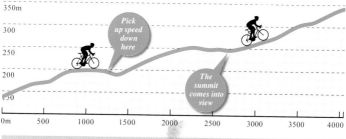

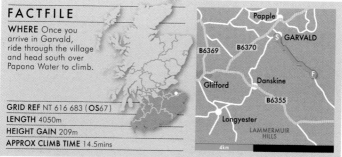

FACTFILE

WHERE Once you arrive in Garvald, ride through the village and head south over Papana Water to climb.

GRID REF NT 616 683 (OS67)

LENGTH 4050m

HEIGHT GAIN 209m

APPROX CLIMB TIME 14.5mins

STOW HILL

STOW, SCOTTISH BORDERS

The hard work on this climb lies at the bottom, as you pull yourself up and away from Stow. Bending left to head into some trees, you pass a warning of the 15% gradient ahead. The sign slightly undersells the severity of the next 500 metres, though – it is a proper struggle to break free of their confines and leave the punishing beginning behind. But once through, assuming you haven't done too much damage to your legs, the rest of the climb is comparatively easy, and punctuated briefly by a levelling. As the 5% slope continues its journey to the serenity at the summit you may be tempted to engage the big ring, but every now and again there is a slight increase in the pitch to remind you that, actually, that's not a good idea. Once you pass the last of the trees and cross a cattle grid the empty summit appears on a blissfully featureless horizon, where you finish in wonderful solitude.

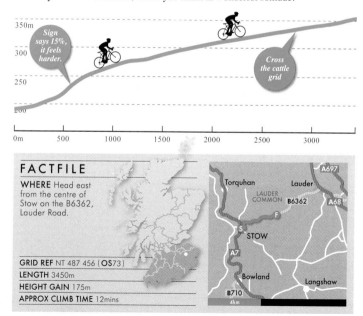

FACTFILE

WHERE Head east from the centre of Stow on the B6362, Lauder Road.

GRID REF NT 487 456 (OS73)
LENGTH 3450m
HEIGHT GAIN 175m
APPROX CLIMB TIME 12mins

CASTLE GATE

JEDBURGH, SCOTTISH BORDERS

Castle Gate heads south-west from Jedburgh and its toughest climbing can be found on the lower slopes. On passing the castle that gives the road its name you reach a 9% sign – if you hadn't already started to feel the gradient in your legs, this warning will certainly draw your attention to it (and rub it in further if you had). The slope continues to be a struggle for some time; passing between tall hedgerows in a dead straight line, you grind up and up. Thankfully, a kink in direction towards the entrance to the golf club affords you some rest. Levelling and then dipping down slightly, you can gather yourself here for the finale. Over to your left are some radio masts sat on top of the hill, but the climb's summit lies in the gap cut into the trees to your right. The road weaves its way through the fields on a slope that is a degree or so easier than it was lower down, then plateaus between the trees at the base of the track leading to the masts.

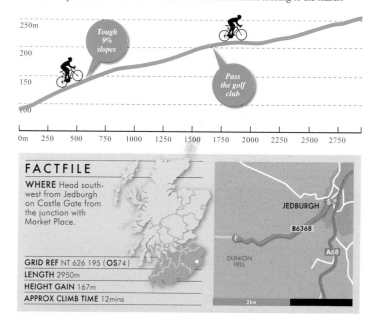

Tough 9% slopes

Pass the golf club

250m

200

150

100

0m 250 500 750 1000 1250 1500 1750 2000 2250 2500 2750

FACTFILE

WHERE Head south-west from Jedburgh on Castle Gate from the junction with Market Place.

JEDBURGH

B6368

DUNION HILL

A68

2km

GRID REF NT 626 195 (OS74)

LENGTH 2950m

HEIGHT GAIN 167m

APPROX CLIMB TIME 12mins

WAUCHOPE FOREST

SAUGHTREE, SCOTTISH BORDERS

I found this climb by accident, and it is so brilliant I just had to include it in the book. Tracking the course of the river and running parallel to the English border, the road climbs gently to begin with on an almost non-existent gradient. It begins to bite once you cross a cattle grid and the road heads east, slicing through the interlocking hills on its journey to the forest. When the tree-covered summit appears over the horizon the bends become more pronounced, and it is now that you realise you are climbing, leaving the valley behind on your way to the first of two summits. OK, a climb cannot have two summits, but press on across the approaching plateau and plunge down through the thick forest as there is plenty more altitude to be gained ahead. Following a couple of tight bends that will rob you of some of your momentum, you have the hardest kilometre of climbing, up to the true summit and its wonderful views.

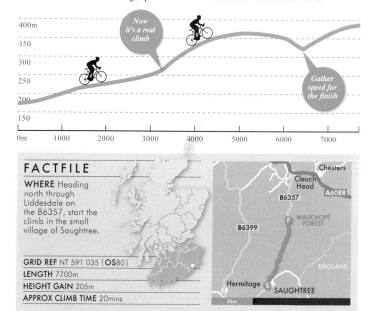

FACTFILE

WHERE Heading north through Liddesdale on the B6357, start the climb in the small village of Saughtree.

GRID REF NT 591 035 (OS80)

LENGTH 7700m

HEIGHT GAIN 205m

APPROX CLIMB TIME 20mins

TINNIS HILL

NEWCASTLETON, SCOTISH BORDERS

The road in the picture opposite may look pan flat, but trust me, it is uphill, just only very, very slightly. It is a different story on the lower slopes though. Leaving Newcastleton, bending left then sweeping right, it turns into a serious 7% grind for almost two kilometres. Weaving a little between the sparse grassland, where you will notice many subtle changes in gradient, you reach a cattle grid, at which point the complexion of the road changes. Meandering on a much kinder slope, you come to the start of three amazing kilometres of arrow-straight road set on the very slightest of gradients. If the wind is on your back, you will be able to stick it in the big ring and pound your way up. If it is in your face, this slope will feel like 10% and you will grovel at a snail's pace. Heading for Tinnis Hill on the horizon, you turn right at its base and, on a slightly stiffer slope, continue your quest to the top for a further two kilometres.

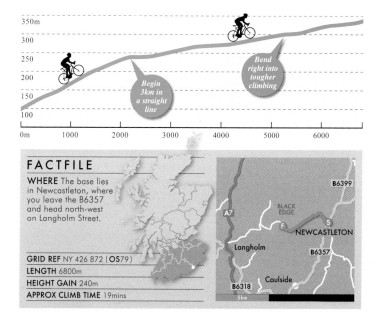

FACTFILE

WHERE The base lies in Newcastleton, where you leave the B6357 and head north-west on Langholm Street.

GRID REF NY 426 872 (OS79)

LENGTH 6800m

HEIGHT GAIN 240m

APPROX CLIMB TIME 19mins

THE WALL OF TALLA

TWEEDSMUIR, SCOTTISH BORDERS

I had heard a lot about this magnificent climb before I rode it, mainly from people that were astonished I had failed to include it in *100 Greatest Cycling Climbs*. It sits on a road that, when ridden from the east, takes you through one of the most beautiful valleys in Britain. But to climb the Wall of Talla, you must ride in from the west. Following the edge of the Talla Reservoir on my way to the base, I spied what looked like a road cutting up the hillside ahead. 'No, it can't be,' I thought. 'It's way too steep, that would just be silly!' But as I drew closer, it dawned on me – this was indeed the road. Right from its bottom corner, the narrow sliver of tarmac rockets skyward, hitting 20% almost right away, and it continues in this vein up to the small bridge crossing the reservoir. The second half is thankfully much more gentle, but with broken legs it will hurt just as much, and you will be toiling all the way to the summit.

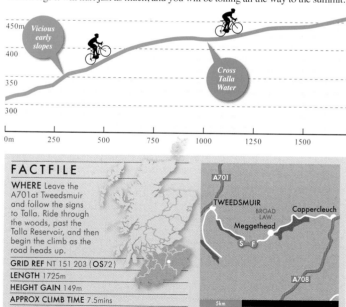

Vicious early slopes

Cross Talla Water

FACTFILE

WHERE Leave the A701 at Tweedsmuir and follow the signs to Talla. Ride through the woods, past the Talla Reservoir, and then begin the climb as the road heads up.

GRID REF NT 151 203 (**OS72**)

LENGTH 1725m

HEIGHT GAIN 149m

APPROX CLIMB TIME 7.5mins

A701

TWEEDSMUIR
BROAD LAW
Cappercleuch
Meggethead
S F

A708

5km

DEVIL'S BEEF TUB

MOFFAT, DUMFRIES AND GALLOWAY

What is remarkable about this climb is its unnerving ability to stick to virtually the same gradient from base to summit, all 10 kilometres of it. Head out of Moffat on the A701, the scenic route to Edinburgh, and begin your ascent once past the town sign. You will hardly notice the rise at first as you wind solidly through the gently following bends. The road sways left and right, never drastically changing direction, just meandering onwards and upwards. At the junction with the B719 you reach the only real change in gradient, a levelling up to a pair of bends, right and then left. Once past these you will see the beautiful hills that line the horizon, effortlessly morphing into one another, as smooth and soft as giant green pillows. The equally smooth road continues to snake along, climbing continuously and getting steeper round the side of the hill overlooking the Beef Tub. Eventually, the climb evaporates and you level to the finish.

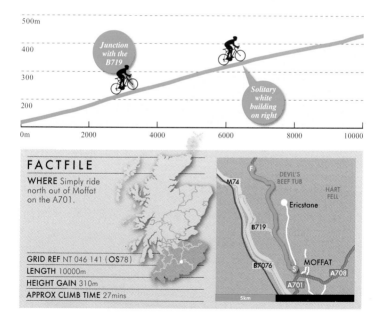

FACTFILE

WHERE Simply ride north out of Moffat on the A701.

GRID REF NT 046 141 (OS78)

LENGTH 10000m

HEIGHT GAIN 310m

APPROX CLIMB TIME 27mins

MENNOCK PASS

MENNOCK, DUMFRIES AND GALLOWAY

Home to Wanlockhead, the highest village in Scotland, the Mennock Pass links the A76 and the A74(M) over the top of the Lowther Hills. The beauty of this route when ridden from the Mennock side has to be seen to be believed. Begin the climb from the pan-flat, wide valley floor, whose smooth, steep sides tower above you. The gradient of the pass picks up on its way through the huddled hills, winding from the base of one to the base of the next. Across a stone bridge the road climbs steeper, cutting its way upwards. There is a small, sinuous downhill around midway, and when an antiquated guard rail swaps from the right to the left side of the road it gets steep again. This is a really long climb, never too steep but constantly challenging. By the time you reach Wanlockhead you have all but conquered the Mennock Pass, but there is just a little bit more to do – ride through the village before the road starts to head downhill.

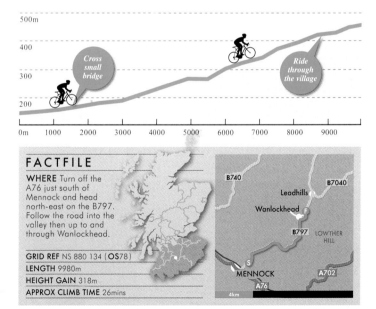

FACTFILE

WHERE Turn off the A76 just south of Mennock and head north-east on the B797. Follow the road into the valley then up to and through Wanlockhead.

GRID REF NS 880 134 (**OS**78)

LENGTH 9980m

HEIGHT GAIN 318m

APPROX CLIMB TIME 26mins

SOUTHERN SCOTLAND   **129**

LOWTHER HILL

WANLOCKHEAD, DUMFRIES AND GALLOWAY

Any big race organisers out there looking for the perfect mountaintop finish, look no further. If you add on the ascent of the Mennock Pass, you get almost 14 kilometres of fabulous climbing through truly awesome scenery. Leave the B797 just outside of Wanlockhead: take the right-hand turn, negotiate the gate at the base, and then start your effort to reach the radar at the top. The initial slopes are gentle, twisting through the silence of the rolling hills. Then there is a stiff 100 metre stretch followed by a faint dip, from where you will see a tower on the horizon. The closer you get to this, the tougher and more Alpine the climb becomes, with countless bends and stunning views. The tower does not sit at the top, though – you must press on, up the perpetually tough slope, until you reach the giant golf ball-shaped radar that lies in the clouds, just waiting for cyclists to find it.

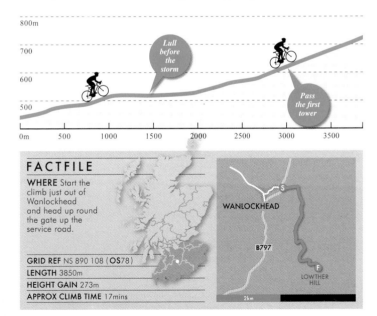

800m
700
600
500

Lull before the storm

Pass the first tower

0m   500   1000   1500   2000   2500   3000   3500

FACTFILE

WHERE Start the climb just out of Wanlockhead and head up round the gate up the service road.

WANLOCKHEAD

B797

S

F

LOWTHER HILL

2km

GRID REF NS 890 108 (OS78)

LENGTH 3850m

HEIGHT GAIN 273m

APPROX CLIMB TIME 17mins

GUFFOCK HILL

A dead end, but well worth including in a ride around these parts, the climb up to Guffock Hill is set on a consistently arduous gradient from base to summit. There are a handful of slight variations, but on the whole you will manage with a couple of gears all the way – which ones depends on which way the wind is blowing. Take the minor road heading north from the B740 to begin the climb. Cross the railway line and aim for the small woods on the hillside. Although the slope may be uniform in pitch, the road surface is not – what starts out well maintained and smooth becomes distinctly rough after the cattle grid at approximately half way. Bending right and left to follow the contours of the hillside, the road is adorned with patches of grass. Towards the top, if you like a bit of rough, you can treat yourself to some off-road and gain a further 25 metres in altitude, up to the masts of Todholes Hill.

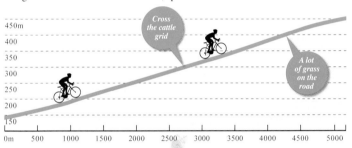

Cross the cattle grid

A lot of grass on the road

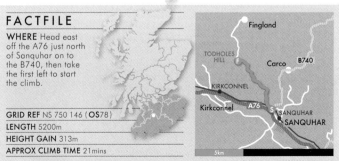

FACTFILE

WHERE Head east off the A76 just north of Sanquhar on to the B740, then take the first left to start the climb.

GRID REF NS 750 146 (**OS**78)

LENGTH 5200m

HEIGHT GAIN 313m

APPROX CLIMB TIME 21mins

CAMBRET HILL

The picture on the left doesn't tell the whole story of this climb, but this is what awaits you at the top: a kilometre of wild, steep, climbing with, I expect, great views. As you can see, when I rode it, all I got was cloud. Begin the climb in the village of Creetown and head up the narrow Minnipool Place. The quiet road rises gently between the surrounding fields, connecting various farms on its way. At this point there is little indication of the trials ahead but, following a slight dip through the woods and across a steam, the gradient increases. The second half of the climb is noticeably harder, creeping closer to the ever-present radio masts on the peak ahead. Crossing a cattle grid you now reach the right turning to the summit and begin the astonishing finale. The now rough and broken road twists across the moorland, getting steeper and steeper all the way to the finish.

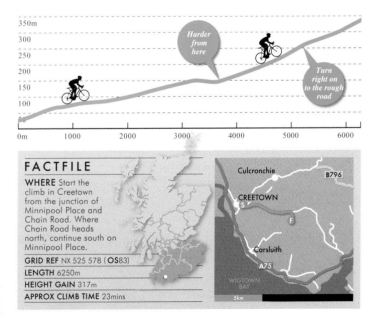

FACTFILE

WHERE Start the climb in Creetown from the junction of Minnipool Place and Chain Road. Where Chain Road heads north, continue south on Minnipool Place.

GRID REF NX 525 578 (**OS**83)

LENGTH 6250m

HEIGHT GAIN 317m

APPROX CLIMB TIME 23mins

RATING 6/10

BROWN CARRICK HILL

AYR, SOUTH AYRSHIRE

To the south-west of Ayr lies the solitary peak of Brown Carrick Hill, and luckily
for us there is a road that runs right to the top of it. Tough from either side, I chose the
more straightforward north face, riding away from the coast and the A719 towards
the mound ahead. From the off you will see the road laid out for all to see, heading up
to the left of the three radio masts that adorn the summit. You climb gently through
farmland and then, following a brace of bends, the required effort intensifies. Up to a
large white farmhouse, across a cattle grid, and into a jumble of twists and turns, 10%
soon turns into 15% and the corners get tighter. Upon reaching open grassland it is
now time to take the right turn, navigate the gate, and push for the top. Ahead lies the
wonderful access road to the summit: smooth, quiet and with six wonderful bends –
a joy to climb, and justly rewarded with uninterrupted views out to sea.

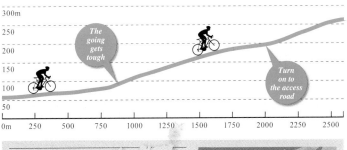

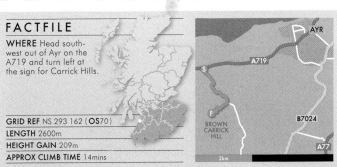

FACTFILE

WHERE Head south-west out of Ayr on the A719 and turn left at the sign for Carrick Hills.

GRID REF NS 293 162 (**OS**70)

LENGTH 2600m

HEIGHT GAIN 209m

APPROX CLIMB TIME 14mins

NICK OF THE BALLOCH

BALLOCH, SOUTH AYRSHIRE

What an absolute beauty this road is. I had no idea what to expect when I arrived, and I was gobsmacked. It is a climb you will want to ride again and again; a climb on which you will want to take your time so you can soak it all in. Starting from the T-junction between North and South Balloch the slope gradually ramps up until you hit the toughest part of the ride, which is close to 20% at the apex. It continues hard past the entrance to the Galloway Forest Park, and then, after a right-hand corner, eases back – it is never too challenging again. After snaking through the forest you will see the marvellous valley open up to your right, and from here on it is simply stunning. The twisting barrier tracing the path of the road, juxtaposed with the pristine beauty it sits in, merely emphasises the drama of this climb. Weaving between the barren peaks, you eventually summit at the Nick, which divides the interlocking hills.

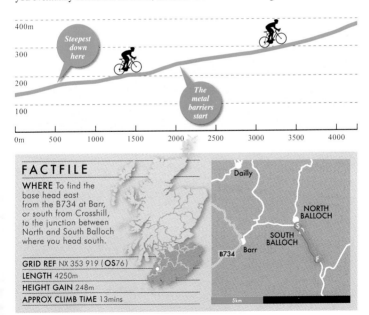

FACTFILE

WHERE To find the base head east from the B734 at Barr, or south from Crosshill, to the junction between North and South Balloch where you head south.

GRID REF NX 353 919 (OS76)

LENGTH 4250m

HEIGHT GAIN 248m

APPROX CLIMB TIME 13mins

RIDE THEM ALL

LEAVE THE LOW ROADS AND HEAD FOR THE HIGH ROADS

No matter where your starting point, many of these 60 brilliant climbs will take a considerable effort to reach, as they are to be found in the furthest corners of Britain. If you have already been filling in the checklists in the original *100 Greatest Cycling Climbs* and its sequel, *Another 100 Greatest Cycling Climbs*, then you can cross those you have ridden off first and see where you need to head next. Make some plans, pack your best waterproofs, including a good plastic bag for the book, and head north. Best of luck!

HIGHLANDS

Hill	Date Ridden	Time
Quinag		
Glen Loth		
Beinn nam Ban		
An Teallach		
Struie Hill		
Bealach na Bà		
Quiraing		
Ben Grasco		
Glen Brittle		
Bealach Udal		
Bealach Ratagan		
Glengarry		
Bealach Feith Nan Laogh		
Beinn nam Beathrach		
McBain Hill		
Glen Kyllachy		

	Date Ridden	Time
Carn an t-Suidhe		
Cairn Gorm		
Glen Coe		
Glen Etive		

EAST SCOTLAND

Hill	Date Ridden	Time
Califer Hill		
The Lecht		
Crathie Hill		
Cairn o'Mount		
Cairnwell Pass		
Craigowl Hill		
Pitroddie Hill		
Abernethy Glen		
Dunning Common		
Cleish Hill		
Purin Hill		
Trinafour Hill		
Ben Lawers		
Kenmore Hill		
Glen Quaich		

WEST SCOTLAND

Hill	Date Ridden	Time
Lairig Nan Lunn Road		

Duke's Pass		
Crow Road		
Tak-Ma-Doon Road		
Rest and Be Thankful		
Glen Finart		
Bealach Maim		
The Serpentine		
Lyle Hill		
Fairlie Moor		
Dervaig Hill		
Ben More Road		

SOUTHERN SCOTLAND

Hill	Date Ridden	Time
White Castle		
Stow Hill		
Castle Gate		
Wauchope Forest		
Tinnis Hill		
The Wall of Talla		
Devil's Beef Tub		
Mennock Pass		
Lowther Hill		
Guffock Hill		
Cambret Hill		
Brown Carrick Hill		
Nick of the Balloch		

Ride them all.

WWW.100CLIMBS.CO.UK

BRITISH CLIMBING GUIDES ALREADY AVAILABLE

GREATEST CYCLING CLIMBS
A ROAD CYCLIST'S GUIDE TO BRITAIN'S HILLS
SIMON WARREN

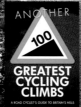

ANOTHER
GREATEST CYCLING CLIMBS
A ROAD CYCLIST'S GUIDE TO BRITAIN'S HILLS
SIMON WARREN

CYCLING CLIMBS OF SOUTH-EAST ENGLAND
A ROAD CYCLIST'S GUIDE

CYCLING CLIMBS OF YORKSHIRE
A ROAD CYCLIST'S GUIDE
SIMON WARREN

CYCLING CLIMBS OF WALES
A ROAD CYCLIST'S GUIDE
SIMON WARREN

CYCLING CLIMBS OF THE MIDLANDS
A ROAD CYCLIST'S GUIDE
SIMON WARREN

CYCLING CLIMBS OF SOUTH-WEST ENGLAND
A ROAD CYCLIST'S GUIDE
SIMON WARREN